A CUP OF COMFORT

COMFORT

for

Adoptive Families

Stories that celebrate
a special gift of love

Edited by Colleen Sell

adamsmedia
~on, Massachusetts

For the Dean family:
Tom, Teri, Amy, and Stephanie

A Cup of Comfort® is a registered trademark of F+W Media, Inc.

Published by
Adams Media, a division of F+W Media, Inc.
57 Littlefield Street, Avon, MA 02322 U.S.A.
www.adamsmedia.com and *www.cupofcomfort.com*

ISBN 10: 1-59869-870-2
ISBN 13: 978-1-59869-870-1

Printed in the United States of America.

J I H G F E D C B A

Library of Congress Cataloging-in-Publication Data
is available from the publisher.

Contents

Acknowledgments

Producing an anthology such as this requires the contributions and cooperation of literally thousands of people—from the innumerable kind souls who forward the call for submissions to their colleagues far and wide, to the multitude of brave hearts who send in their stories, to the talented writers who patiently work with me to shape their stories into a compelling and cohesive whole, to the dedicated professionals at Adams Media who produce such excellent books so well, to the media and critics who give the book a nod, to the booksellers who make the book accessible to the public, and especially to the readers, without whom this book would not exist and for whom this book has been crafted.

I am grateful to each and every one of this legion of people, most especially the *Cup of Comfort*® A-Team: Meredith O'Hayre, Paula Munier, Laura Daly, Jacquinn Williams, and Karen Cooper. A tip of the hat also goes to the book's copy editor, Jennifer Bright Reich, and designer, Ashley Vierra.

Introduction

"We witness a miracle every time a child enters into life. But those who make their journey home across time and miles, growing within the hearts of those who wait to love them, are carried on the wings of destiny and placed among us by God's very own hands."

—Kristi Larson

For many, if not most, people, there is no calling more innate, more fervent, more challenging, and more rewarding than parenting a child. And there are literally millions of children, domestically and abroad, who are in need of nurturing, stable, permanent homes. So it is no surprise that, at the last official count, 1.7 million households in the United States included at least one adopted child. What did surprise me is that this number represents only 4 percent of American households and that only about 120,000 children are adopted each year in the United States, while more than 500,000 American children are available for adoption, an estimated 130,000 newborns are relinquished by birth parents in the United States each year, and the number of orphans worldwide continues to rise dramatically. And I suspect the United States is not alone in the disparity between the number of kids who are available and the number of kids who are placed. Why, I can't help but wonder, aren't substantially more of these children being adopted by willing and able adults?

The answer to that question is multifaceted and complicated, and some of the factors are rather disturbing, as I discovered through my research in preparing to compile this anthology of inspiring stories for and about adoptive families. But what that basic research, coupled with reading the more than 1,200 stories submitted for this book, made clear to me is that adopting a child is often a complex, expensive, and difficult process, that adoption is a deeply personal choice, and that each adoption is unique to those individuals and circumstances. I also learned that, even when the adoption experience is difficult, as it sometimes is, it is also considered a blessing by and results in a positive outcome for both the adoptee and the adoptive family as well as for the birth family.

Still, so many children wait for permanent homes with loving, nurturing, stable families. And that troubles me.

So it is my personal hope that this book serves two purposes: the one for which it was initially intended: to celebrate adoptive families, and also to inspire others to adopt a child (or two or three or more). Because every child is truly a miracle. And bringing a child into your heart and into your home is truly God's work.

It has been an honor for me to work with a few of God's miracle workers—the adoptees and their families who have so graciously and skillfully shared their personal experiences in this book. I trust these stories will bring you comfort and joy, insight and inspiration, and a few compassionate tears and a slew of smiles, just as they have to me. Enjoy!

—*Colleen Sell*

Aglow with Gratitude

I tell myself that the sweat doesn't matter, that the black turtleneck I am wearing blends in with the Phoenix, Arizona, asphalt and that the itching around my neck is just to keep me alert. The cramp in my right hamstring that has developed from eight hours of driving and that has now stiffened into a stubborn crunch doesn't matter either. What matters is that I am convinced that my body is full of lights, and I am on my way to the hospital.

Through my windshield, I can see all the workers in their cars on the interstate being guided home by the sun's low rays. For an instant, I consider seeing myself in one of those cars as if I had been raised here all along, as if I had stayed in this city of my birth instead of moving to Los Angeles and to all of the other cities I have lived in over the years. Adopted people tend to think in "what-ifs," I suppose.

The lights inside my body rattle with the rhythm of my car's tires hitting the bumps and cracks in the highway. They are not just any lights, but multicolored bulbs strung together and encased in plastic tulips the shades of pale green, pink, blue, and yellow. They have been inside my body since the moment I began as a child to imagine my biology and what it is like in there, under my skin, inside the parts of me that I cannot see.

Then, one morning a few years ago, I went to the hospital for an endoscopy. After the procedure, the doctor shook me awake as I lay on a hospital gurney and showed me photographs of the inside of my esophagus. "It's dark in there!" I exclaimed. "It's not supposed to be dark in there."

What was I to do with my newfound darkness? Did my lights still exist? Was the darkness bad? Was the darkness doubt, anxiety, fear, vulnerability—or worse, was it the unknown?

As an adopted person, I had spoken to the unknown on a daily basis, actively ignored it or wrestled with it, and sometimes begged it to reveal something to me that I could attach myself to and stick. I learned that the questions most people could answer with certainty I could not answer in the same way. So what's your mom's name? "Gert," I could say, referring to the complex, loud-laughing, wildly left-centered and compassionate woman who had adopted me. My biological mother's name, however, I could not say. Whom do you look like? Answer: the unknown. What is your family history? Answer: the unknown. Where do you belong? Answer: the unknown. Who are you? Answer: I am a woman full of lights.

I reach up and pull my sweater away from my neck, place my skinny fingers against my skin, and begin to scratch. If I could see myself in the rearview mirror, I'd probably see a twisted expression on my face, indicating relief and weariness, and red marks on my skin from the sweat and scratching. I squint at the signs above, looking for the highway loop 202, and grab for the wrinkled piece of paper on which I have written the directions to the hospital where I was born.

I am forty-two years old, and with the exception of the first four months of my life, I have never lived in Arizona. Over the years, whenever I have applied for a passport, I have seen the words "Maricopa County" and "Phoenix" on my birth certificate. Until now, however, I have stayed away from the hospital where I was born. So why visit the Maricopa County Medical Center now? Call it maturity. Call it timing. All I know is that when the moment arrived that I was no longer afraid of what I would find out about myself, it finally pushed me into action, and I pushed fear into the back seat of my Civic and started on this long road to the hospital.

Along the way, somewhere inside my darkness, the realization emerged that, in addition to challenging me, the unknown had been a kind of comfort. After all, it had allowed me to create any story I chose when I defined myself. But what if now, after actually visiting and seeing the place where I was born, I discovered something terrible about myself that I could not deny? What if visiting the place of my birth revealed things about me that I would have no power to change?

I see the exit for North 24th Street and merge to the right and down the off-ramp. I had originally intended to spend the night at a hotel and visit the hospital in the morning when I was refreshed and clean. But a lifetime of wondering propels me forward despite my tiredness and dishevelment, and a feeling of I-just-have-to-know overtakes me.

The hospital is smaller than I had imagined, shaped almost like a multilayered adobe, with an earthy brown color and white trim on the outside. I turn into the driveway and drive past the front entrance and the hospice center and around to the rear of the building. My car hums quietly, as if pleased at driving fast on the open road for so long.

I turn off the engine and look up. My hair sticks to the side of my cheek. I tell myself that I can just stay right here, that I don't really need to go inside, that I can say what I came to say without venturing any further. Still, I open my car door, step outside, and begin to walk. I know it is time.

As it turns out, I am full of light. White light. It enters me as it reflects boldly off the walls of the hospital's second floor maternity ward, the one that displays the large labor and delivery sign that now hangs above my head. The light is bright and unmistakable. It gives me comfort, like lying in a clean, white porcelain bathtub.

Yet, standing here, I am nervous. I dip my hands into the pockets of my loose jeans. I am alone, and I have something to say. I want to say thank you privately, without anyone seeing me from behind the desk or coming at me from around the corner.

With the labor and delivery sign above me, I look to my left and see two large doors. On the other side of the doors, at the end of the hall, is another sign that just reads "Labor." I bow my head and close my eyes, and my eyelashes flutter. I try to remember the words I want to say. The words rush through my silence like rapidly waving lifelines as I grab them one at a time and try to line them up in the correct order. I want them to mean something that I won't ever take back or regret. I want them to be simple. I know this is my one chance to get it right for myself, to say what I need to say. I know this is my original circle coming to a close, and I want to close it with some form of purity.

I open my eyes. I am still alone. I look up to see a security camera above me. I bow my head, anyway, close my eyes again, tap my toe on the floor, and the words finally come. *Thank you for my life*, I say in silent prayer. *Thank you for my life. Thank you to my biological mother and father. Thank you to the hospital staff. Thank you to God for my safe delivery. And, most important, thank you to Harold and Gertrude Israelow for giving me a home, for giving me themselves as my parents. Thank you to all of these. Thank you for my life. With great love and admiration. Amen.*

I hear two toddlers giggling and squirming on the floor in the waiting room behind me. A young boy, about ten years old, sits near them silently. He looks at me through his round glasses. His skin is dark, and his bangs cross over one of his lenses. I wonder if his mother is here giving birth. I turn to look down the hall, and I see the "Labor" sign once again. *Hallelujah!* I think to myself.

As I walk through the halls on my way out, I see many faces of people of color. I am reminded of the story my mother tells me about when the adoption agent called her to tell her that I was available for adoption. "She has some Indian blood, though. Do you mind?" the agent had said.

The lights inside of me are white and clear, some with pointy tips and some with curves like the moon. My darkness is here, too, cushioning the lights, nurturing all the lessons I have yet to learn until they are ripe for lighting.

Before I leave the hospital, I decide to stop at the gift shop located in the lobby. Maybe there will be a memento here for me to take with me, something tangible that I can hold or look at from time to time.

I swing my purse over my shoulder as I walk into the shop. Two ladies stand behind the counter helping customers and talking to each other about celebrities. I look through the small room carefully for something that feels right to hold. I see necklaces and earrings, magazines and small glass sculptures with Biblical writing etched into them. I see T-shirts and snacks.

I am a woman full of lights with my little toe now fixed into the Phoenix earth.

Above me, I see what I unknowingly came into the gift shop to buy. I pull the item off the hook and place it on the counter next to the cash register. My dollar bills crackle as I unfold them from my wallet.

"Would you like a bag for that?" one lady asks me.

I say that I would and "thank you very much."

"I think a pink bag will do just right," she says.

I smile and agree.

The sun envelops me softly as I exit the hospital and walk toward my car. My shoulders are relaxed and lower now as I breathe breaths of shock, breaths of gratitude.

Inside my car, I take the item that I have purchased out of the bag and hold it in my hand. Resting in my palm is a small, clear package. Inside the package is a pair of booties, pink for a newborn baby girl.

—Randi Israelow

A Tale of Two Names

By the time we received our referral information on the little girl from India who would eventually become our daughter, we had already chosen a name: Liya. I'd heard it on a television show once and thought it unique and pretty, and for once my husband agreed. After some research, I tracked down its origins as Hebrew, meaning "I am the Lord's." This somehow felt appropriate for a child who had started her life without a family. And I am a writer, after all, so words, names, and meanings are what I'm all about.

The thick referral packet included pictures, videos, and progress reports of the healthy, beautiful one-year-old as well as her birth name, Gauri. When I first read and fumbled around the pronunciation, "Gar-ee," I'd wrinkled my nose with some distaste and thought it was a good thing we'd already picked out another name. Gauri would do for her middle name to keep a piece of her Eastern Indian heritage, but I couldn't imagine pairing it with our very Dutch surname, "VanBaale."

My first name, Kali, strangely enough, has Hindu ties. Kali is the name of a famous Hindu goddess . . . the goddess of energy and destruction, as my husband so loves to point out. As fun as it was to discover this meaning, I still cringed at how my first and last names phonetically sounded together. Kal-ee Van-Baal-ee. Never mind the endless mispronunciations.

Admittedly, I also struggled with the idea of our child's name being chosen by a complete stranger. Our two older boys are our biological children, and the names we'd chosen for them had meaningful family connections. It was hard at times for us to think that we weren't there on the day our daughter was born and that we'd missed so many of those first-year milestones. We at least wanted to pick out the name she'd carry for the rest of her life.

As with most international adoptions, once we received our referral, it was another ten months before all the legalities were complete and we were cleared to travel to India to get her. During those long months of waiting with updates few and far between, a peculiar thing happened. We never referred to Gauri as Liya. My husband and I, even our boys, called her only Gauri. We proudly showed off her picture to family and friends, introducing her as Gauri. Once, when

I did correct myself and called her Liya, my oldest son looked at me with a confused expression and said, "Who are you talking about?"

One night while lying in bed, my husband confessed that the name Gauri had really started to grow on him. He actually liked it and wanted to know if I was open to keeping it. Even though I'd yet to use the name Liya, my knee-jerk reaction was still "no way." But I promised him I would think about it. The very next day I started yet another search—this time for the origin and meanings of Hindu names. What I found would take my breath away and end any lingering doubts I had that our daughter was meant to be "Gauri."

The story I came across read as follows:

In the Hindu religion, there is a great god named Lord Shiva, the god of war. Lord Shiva was in love with a goddess, Parvati, the lover of life, who brought prowess into the world as she infused it with her magic.

Like most goddesses, Parvati was said to have both mild and terrible aspects and took many different forms. Two of her very fierce and powerful forms were Durga, goddess beyond reach, and Kali, goddess of energy and destruction. As Kali, Parvati used her strength for both evil and good and was often called upon by others during times of need. She was

*able to answer with her ferociousness and fearless-
ness to fight battles.*

*During one such terrible battle, Kali became intoxi-
cated with bloodlust and ran amuck across the three
worlds, destroying everything and everyone in her
sight. To restrain and calm her, Shiva took the form
of a corpse and blocked her path. Kali tripped on
his lifeless body and was jolted from her frenzy.
Devastated and in mourning, Kali placed a foot
on Shiva's chest and brought him back to life. Shiva
then took the form of a little child and began to cry,
stirring maternal love in the heart of Kali. Forced
to shed her fierce form, Kali became the Goddess
Gauri, radiant mother, bestower of life, the goddess
of motherhood and nurturing. So it was that Gauri
made Kali a mother.*

And so it was that our daughter Liya stayed
Gauri, who she was meant to be all along. Now, her
name rolls off my tongue as if I've said it my entire
life, and I can't imagine calling her anything else.
So often adoptions seem destined to be; such is the
case with our story. We are Kali Jo VanBaale and
Gauri Jo VanBaale, and really, it's okay if you mis-
pronounce them both. We don't mind anymore.

—Kali VanBaale

He Has Her Hands, but They Hold My Heart

As a little girl with two younger sisters, I always planned that, when I married, I was only having boys, hopefully a houseful. But God didn't see fit to give my husband, Johnnie, and me sons. Instead, he blessed us with two wonderful, challenging daughters. When Karyn and Melinda were eleven and eight, we decided not to have more children. Instead, we would be foster parents and perhaps adopt a little boy one day.

God, in his infinite wisdom and incomparable wit, saw to it that most of the more than one hundred children we fostered over the next many years were, you guessed it, girls.

When a social worker called and asked us to take a two-month-old boy, it was like he dropped into our lives straight from heaven. Robert came to us skinny, pale, and looking much like the starving orphans we had seen on television, but almost overnight he grew into a robust, cheerful, beautiful little boy, a delight to our whole family. Television sat forgotten in the corner; it couldn't possibly compete with his crinkling black eyes and contagious chuckling. To cause that merry laugh became the goal of everyone in the family.

As foster parents, our express task was to help reunite children with their biological families, and we took that seriously. I faithfully took Robert to every scheduled visit with his teenage mother, but many times she failed to even show up. My heart went out to her older son, only four years old, as well as to the new baby boy she'd given birth to when Robert was thirteen months old; they were always underdressed, filthy, and smelly, with runny noses. Somehow she always managed to keep the two of them just on the fringe of criminal neglect and so retained custody. A fourth child, a girl, born eleven months before Robert, was in another foster home.

There was, we thought, good reason to hope that Robert would be the first foster child we had ever kept who would be placed for adoption. The mother showed little interest in either child in foster care. She had her older and younger sons and was pregnant again as Robert approached his second birthday.

That's when we received the call. Department of Family and Children Services (DFACS) had decided to terminate parental rights on the little girl and allow her to be adopted. However, Robert would start home visits immediately in preparation for going home.

We couldn't believe it! It defied all logic. Surely they knew the home was unsafe for any child, much less the sheltered, secure child that Robert had become. How could they say that it was safe for Robert to go home but not his sister? For that matter, how could they say that any of the children were safe in that environment?

The explanation the social worker gave us was shocking. They had made a deal with the mother. The case had dragged on too long. The judge was pressuring them to resolve the case, and there was a good possibility he would order both children sent back home. So they told her that if she would voluntarily surrender her parental rights to her daughter, who had been in foster care a year longer than Robert, they would give Robert back to her. The little girl was more fragile than Robert, they reasoned. After all, wasn't that better than the judge ordering both children back into the home?

Since becoming foster parents, we'd seen many children leave our home to go back to questionable, even dangerous, situations. It was the most difficult part of a difficult job. People often asked us how we could take in a child, learn to love the child as our own, and then just let them go. For us, it was simple. We did it for the children. Each leave-taking brought its own misery. But during their time with us, we did what we could. We were willing to break our own hearts so that we could give a child a safe harbor, love, and acceptance for whatever time we had with them. For some, that brief time would be the only "normal" childhood they would ever know.

I knew the rules: This is not your child. You are not the parent. You are only a temporary placement. We were forbidden to contact the children after they left us, unless the parent chose to contact us.

But when Robert left, something pulled at me to know where he was. I found myself praying for him, driving down the street where I knew his young mother and the children lived, trying to catch a glimpse of him. I came armed with gifts for all the children, my ticket in the door. Every eleven months or so, there was a new baby.

Robert always came to me eagerly. Sometimes, his mother would allow me to take him for hamburgers or back to our house to see the rest of the family. He even spent the night with us a few times during the first year after he left us. Many times as I drove him back, he cried and begged to stay with us. It was agony to make him go back. I often saw bruises, and he was always dirty. But he soon learned to be brave, to not let her see him cry; otherwise, she would be angry and might not let us see him again.

During the next two years, they moved more than twenty times. Apparently, every time the rent came due, she moved. Often I would drive by and find the children's things strewn about the muddy yard, abandoned, even run over, in their mother's haste to move on before the rent came due. But I always managed to track them down, until, after three years of following, I finally lost them.

I tried to believe it was for the best. In my heart of hearts, I knew Robert was too young to understand why he had to go back every time. Each separation was another abandonment.

Two years went by. Many nights I lay awake wondering where he was, if he was safe, if I would ever see him again. I watched for his golden head and crinkling eyes as I walked through Wal-Mart or the grocery store. And I prayed for him.

Then, late one night, a social worker called. They were taking all the children in Robert's family into foster care. Although she couldn't remember which of the seven children we'd kept before, she wondered if we wanted him back.

We did.

Robert returned to us in January 1995, when he was almost seven years old. He had changed so much, and yet when I looked into his eyes, recognition looked back. He walked around our house, touching things, remembering. He was home.

A year later, the court finally terminated parental rights on all the children, and they were placed for adoption. Robert, now eight, was finally ours for good.

Robert's birth mother went to prison for the things she did and allowed to be done to her children. I don't like to think what they were; I'm not sure anyone will ever know the whole story. There were months of nightmares and disjointed horror stories of "bo-bos" (monsters), blood, drugs, and drunken brawls as Robert fought to free himself and to believe it was really over. Thank God, he doesn't remember everything yet. For a long time he was afraid of his other mother. He knew he had been sent back once. What if it happened again?

"What if she comes after me, Mom? What will we do?"

"I will never let her touch you again, sweetheart. No matter what."

But as he grew, his birth mother's image shrunk. Slowly, he outgrew his fear.

Robert is fifteen now, tall and strong, loving and sensitive. Though he doesn't have my eyes or his daddy's curly hair, he is the son I always wanted in every way. When he hears a comment that Melinda looks like me or that Karyn looks like Daddy or Papa or Aunt Lorraine, he knows that he doesn't.

He asked once, "Who do I look like, Mom?"

Instead of launching into a discussion of heredity and the gene pool, I gave him an honest answer, "You look a lot like Matt, son." Somehow, he does look a little like Melinda's husband, so he was satisfied. Sometimes the simple answer is best, however illogical.

But there is someone else that he looks much more like. And I've always known who that is. When I look at my son's hands, the slender, artistic fingers, and at his fine-boned face, I don't see my own or his daddy's. I see, instead, a tiny girl of about eighteen, barefoot, in cutoff jeans and an old T-shirt. She is standing in DFACS, holding her son for the first time since he'd come to our foster home. She smiles into his eyes, and he smiles back. His face is hers. Those hands are hers.

When Robert came to us as an infant, we had three teenaged foster girls in our home as well as our own two girls. The day we met him, the caseworker might have, instead, called and asked us to take a seventeen-year-old girl who was mother to three children she couldn't take care of. I would have said yes. And we—Johnnie and I—would have loved her, taught her, and fought for her, just as we have for her son, who is now our son.

These days, as I watch my son grow into a fine young man, I thank God every day for sending him into our lives. And my thoughts reach out to that girl whose body nurtured and gave birth to my son. God has helped me to forgive her for the mistakes she made, the times she hurt him and neglected him. She was a child raising children, after all. These days, when my precious son leans down to kiss me good night, I reach to brush his hair, damp from the shower, out of his eyes.

"Aw, Mom, you messed it up!" he says. Grinning, he shakes his hair right back into his eyes, and I smile.

I am profoundly grateful to see her hair. It is that woman-child, the other mother, whose unique genes gave my son his face, his extraordinary ear for music, his eye for drawing, his incredible gift of mimicry, and more.

I like to think that he got some good things from his daddy and me, too. Like all adoptive parents, I wonder sometimes about nature versus nurture. In the end, though, I can only hope that our son is the best of all of us. So I thank God for all the things that make him who he is. And I wouldn't change a thing.

—*Linda Darby Hughes*

A Good Mom

I'm eighteen years old, and this year I started my freshman year of college. I had everything all planned out for myself: college, career, meeting and marrying my soul mate, a house with the traditional white picket fence, kids, everything. It was the perfect dream. Then I found out I was pregnant, and I knew all my plans were about to change, whether I wanted them to or not.

I'll be honest—at first I was horrified. How could this have happened? It didn't seem possible. We'd taken precautions, but sometimes precautions fail. Sometimes God has different plans, and your life can take a very different path than anything you'd ever imagined. Sometimes God decides it is time for you to have a baby.

In the beginning, the very idea of being pregnant scared me to death. I just didn't feel ready for the responsibility. I didn't have my own life figured out; how in the world could I care for another human being?

Worse was the fact that, before I found out I was pregnant, I had done some drinking and inhaled quite a bit of secondhand smoke from my chain-smoking boyfriend. I was wracked with the guilt of possibly having harmed this innocent little life growing inside me. Thank God, my doctor was soon able to put my mind to rest by running tests and assuring me the baby was developing normally, but I still felt like an unfit mother from the start.

I spent a lot of nights alone, crying my eyes out in my dorm room. I didn't have anyone's shoulder to lean on. I hadn't told any of my friends about my situation, and my boyfriend was not an option for support. He proved to be as immature as I'd always suspected. He disappeared before I was through my first trimester, and I never saw him again.

Luckily for my sanity and safety, I was blessed with one of the world's most wonderful moms. I didn't have much time to panic before she stepped in to take care of everything. I have never felt such relief as the day she said, "Honey, why don't you come live with us?"

From that day on, she has been my greatest supporter. She keeps me company when I do errands, she listens whenever I need to talk, and she volunteered to be my Lamaze partner. She always reminds me to exercise and take my vitamins, but she never nags. She just offers to go for walks around the neighborhood with me, or she'll take a vitamin herself and that reminds me to be mindful of my health and the health of my baby.

If I need anything from the store, she volunteers to drive into town to get it, even when it's some crazy craving. Half the time, it seems like she knows exactly what I'll want even before my stomach has made up its mind. She comes home from the store with fried chicken and gallons of mint chocolate ice cream, and I think, *That's exactly it!* She always knows just what I need, even when it's ridiculous. For a few weeks I had to have gummy bears and bologna every night, but she never laughed. She just munched along with me as we sat on the couch together, watching movies late at night when I couldn't sleep.

I guess it was somewhere in my second trimester that I realized I was no longer upset at the idea of having a child. The changes in my body are so amazing, and the baby will be the greatest miracle I can imagine. How could I be upset about that? It seems like years ago that the idea of having a baby caused me such stress. Make no mistake: I realize it won't all be easy. But I know that whenever a child is born into a house filled with love, everything will work out for the best.

Some days I feel like I'm taking advantage of her generosity or that I'm causing too much of a burden on the family. Like when my car got mysteriously washed overnight or when I found beautiful, brand-new maternity clothes laid out on my bed when I got home from the doctor's office.

But whenever I feel like I am taking too much, she simply says, "Family takes care of family," and gives me a big hug, and I am awed and humbled by her generosity once again.

She does all the things I know my own mother would do if she were here. But Laura's not my mom; my parents died when I was little. Until a few months ago, Laura was a complete stranger to me. I am so blessed and so grateful to have been welcomed into her family . . . for Laura is the woman I've chosen to be my baby's adoptive mother.

This was the biggest decision I've ever made, but I know it's the right thing to do. I'm too young and I'm just not ready. I know in my heart that this is the right woman and the right family to take care of my baby.

Laura and her husband have one biological child of their own, a beautiful, inquisitive three-year-old girl. They've always wanted her to have a brother or sister, but Laura's first delivery was to be her last. The doctors said that because of complications, it would not be safe for her to carry another child.

Life is so funny. Just a few short months ago, I was filled with terror at the thought of my body creating a baby. Now, it fills me with sadness to think that there are women out there who cannot do so. With every day that I spend in this house, my conviction becomes stronger that I have found the right home for my child. If I can fill the space in a mother's heart, I've done my job right.

Whenever I'm worried or upset, Laura's wise words always keep me focused on this journey of childbirth, which is hands-down the most important thing I've ever done. She once told me that to be a good mother is to be more concerned with your child's life than with your own. And when I look into the warm, loving eyes of the sweet woman I have chosen to raise my son, I know for certain that I am a good mom.

—*Jessica Pierce*

Souls Speak

I kiss my son goodnight. He is fast asleep, arms around his Ugly Doll, stuffed animals gathered all around him. I touch his thick brown hair that loses itself to waviness if it isn't kept short. I kiss his closed eyelids that cover brown eyes, so dark the pupils are rarely seen. I kiss his nose, its shape beginning to emerge as the cartilage and bone come into formation, defining his proud heritage. Last, I kiss his sweet lips, just rosy-red enough to stand out from his olive, sun-bronzed skin. The dimple in his left cheek is hiding now, only because his ever-busy mouth and expressive face are still. He is a handsome boy, but the beautiful spark—the essence of him—recharges as he sleeps.

He is my youngest. He is the affirmation that God has made a great effort to bring us together. Is my precious son aware, even in the smallest pinpoint of his subconscious, that he is where he is meant to be? I am, and it humbles me.

My son came to me in dreams, little wispy yearnings growing larger and more insistent until I could no longer ignore them. It culminated in November of that year. I had had an emotional week, crying over just about anything. I felt full and raw. It was the emotional sensation of being pregnant. My husband and I were in Chicago, taking a quarterly weekend break from our son and daughters. While waiting for dinner, amidst the Latin music, margaritas, and bar conversations, I blurted out to Mark that I wanted another baby and tearfully asked him to please consider having another.

The direction of the conversation was surreal. It was emotionally wrenching. The discourse was full of surprises for both of us. You see, I didn't plan this exchange; I had never gotten beyond thinking that all I wanted was another baby. I answered my husband's questions, not knowing from where the answers originated. I felt as though I was being guided to answer, and all of the answers just popped into my head, without any forethought.

Mark, taken aback, asked me, "Where do you think this baby is?"

I heard myself say, "Guatemala."

"Why?" he asked.

Shaking my head, I said, "I don't know, I just do."

He paused, really looking at me, "And what do you think this baby is?"

"A boy." I smiled at him through my tears.

"A boy?"

"Yep." I had his full attention now.

Silence from my husband, and then, "Has he been born?"

Wow. This one threw me, but the answer came with certainty, "He has or he will be soon."

That surprised him; me too. I felt my child's soul doing everything it could to get my attention. And I was sharing all of it with Mark.

My husband didn't say no; it would've been hard to. I had unintentionally ambushed him there in the restaurant with hysterical tears. He said he would think about it and that I should just leave him alone with it for a while. I was more than willing to give him the time. I felt very hopeful.

Two weeks passed. Holden, our oldest, came into my upstairs bath to tell me, "Dad said to tell you yes."

I walked out into the hallway where Mark stood. He was crying.

"Is this about the baby?" I asked him.

Nodding, Mark drew me into the circle of his arms. Holding me tightly, he said, "I don't know what's going on. I went into Holden's room saying I needed to talk to him about something important, something that affected our family. He asked if it was about his baby brother. I don't understand this, but somehow Holden is connected in all of this. You need to start the paperwork."

Here's the thing—neither Mark nor I had been talking to our son or daughters about the possibility of another child.

Paperwork was completed very quickly; it was our third international adoption. We began The Wait. Familiar with the process, we settled in for what we thought would be months of waiting for a referral. But, just two weeks after submitting paperwork to our agency, I received a phone call from our agency director. "Are you dossier-ready?"

"Yes," I said.

She knew we were, so I found the question alarming. Starting to panic, I asked, "Has some of our paperwork been lost?"

Paperwork does get lost from time to time. There was so much of it for each of our adoptions. The FBI lost our fingerprints within the first week for this adoption, and we had had to be reprinted.

"No. It's complete. Would you be ready to act on a referral if one came?" she asked.

"Absolutely! Something soon, you think?" I asked.

"I might have something soon."

But we were coming into the holidays and so anticipated that the process would be slowing down significantly. Beating around the bush, she asked me what I was doing. As it turned out, my oldest daughter and I had just returned from gymnastics. She was sleeping soundly in her car seat. It was very odd. The agency director said we would talk again soon.

We said goodbye, and immediately upon hanging up, Mark called. I began to tell him about the phone call when he cut me off saying, "Hold on, I have someone on the other line." When he got back on with me, so was the agency director. She asked me if I was parked, and I assured her that I was. She had our referral and had emailed a picture of the baby to our home. Mark and I told her that we wanted the baby. We didn't need to see a picture to know. She insisted that we get home and look at the file she had emailed to us. She wouldn't accept our answer until we had read the file and seen the baby's picture.

Mark and I met at home. The computer was on and, true to his word, Mark had not opened the file. We wanted to see the baby for the first time together. We opened the file. The information was all there, along with the picture. There he was, a beautiful baby boy, less than a month old. Of course we wanted him. There was never any doubt. He was born in Guatemala, on November 6, during the week that I was so full and raw, on my mother-in-law's birthday.

Our son finally came home when he was eleven months old. He attached to me like Velcro. The bonding with his siblings was profound and immediate. He had a wonderfully strong personality, full of passion and constant energy.

I close the door on my sleeping son—a blessing from God with a vibrant heart-searing soul who came in search of us before he was born. I heard my sweet boy. I was listening.

—*Judy Miller*

Don't Eat My Birth Mother

"Don't eat my birth mother," my five-year-old daughter, Rose, says as I pull a cereal box off of the shelf before pouring. It wasn't just any cereal.

Let me back up and explain. Rose and I received an invitation to a birth mother's brunch a few days earlier. It is a day to honor the place of birth mothers.

"What do I do?" I asked my friend Beth, figuring that she, as an adoptee, adoptive parent, and adoption social worker, might have some wisdom to share.

Silence.

"Is this the kind of thing I tell her we're going to because I think it's important? Or do I let her decide?" I prodded.

"Good question," she said, adding not another word.

There is no book to which I can refer these questions and situations.

I am grateful for this invitation, though, happy we live in a time when adoptive mothers don't pretend birth mothers don't exist. We don't demonize or minimize their role nor presume to speak for them. However, we are still in the deep end of the pool when these issues come up, and I'm not a trained lifeguard.

The invitation is a blessing, too, because it offers me a chance to remind my daughter that her story, although uniquely her own, is shared by others. Rose is not the only person who was birthed, relinquished, and adopted. Rose is not the only girl who does not remember her birth mother. A birth mother brunch acknowledges that our family story is also part of the human story—personal, yes, but also global, shared.

"Why can't we just celebrate at our own house?" Rose asks.

"We can," I say, "make it more private."
"And what about Daddy? Why can't he come?"
"Well, it's a mother and daughter event," I say.
"What about my birth father?" Rose asks.

This is a new era in adoption, where it is not uncommon for the birth father to be acknowledged by all in the adoption triad.

"We can light a candle the day before Father's Day," I say and confess to Rose how I think of my own biological father, a man who left before my first birthday, every Father's Day.

Rose stares at me and then hops off her chair.

"Put your hand up," she says.

I do, and Rose slaps me with an energetic high-five, saying, "I don't know my birth father, either." She exudes the enthusiasm of someone ready to scream "bingo!" We are in the "Oh my God, me, too" realm, and I want to laugh out loud, as I've never received a gleeful response to the "I don't know my biological father" sentence.

Rose is tickled, delighted, overjoyed, and I realize why the "you aren't alone" feeling is potent. Most of us ache for validation. We want a pass into the "me too" club that takes the edge off our losses and proves we are human.

Rose sits down again and starts eating the samoling I'd promised the night before, though I am protective of this food. It's a high-cost and high-protein food that is low-fat and tastes good, which makes it a rare treat for me. Rose, with 1 percent body fat, doesn't need this cereal, but I pour some out on the table in front of her.

She plays with the clusters of granola as we talk.

"She's got long hair—as long as yours," Rose says as the cereal morphs into a crunchy vision of her birth mother.

"But hers would be black," I say.

"Or pink," she says, "so she can go to the Land of Pink." We talk about what it's like in the Land of Pink (everything pink, of course). Her birth mother has enough pink to enter. So does she. I do too. In this imaginary place, we can all be together.

"Don't touch her," Rose says as she leaves the cereal art of her birth mother on the table.

A little while later, Rose climbs into my lap and asks, "Did you get adopted? Does everyone not know their birth mother?"

I explain that my birth mother is the one I call "Mom," the one she knows as "Nana."

She asks if my sister is adopted.

"No," I say, understanding that Rose is realizing not everyone is adopted or separated from their birth mother.

Rose wants to go through the long list of all the people we know to learn who is and who is not adopted.

Rose tells me she is sad and misses her birth mother. I hold her and acknowledge that it *is* sad to talk about her birth mother.

She goes back to the dining room table.

"I love my birth mother as much as I love you." Rose looks up at me a little scared, as though I might be mad.

"I'm glad," I say and kiss her on the head. "I love her, too—for creating you." I am surprised by my own grace. "Do you wish you knew her?" I ask then.

"Does she know my birthday?"

"Yes. She was there on the day you were born."

"Does she know how old I am?"

Again, unlike most questions Rose asks about her birth mother, who lives in China—where it is illegal to abandon a child and where impoverished families are financially punished for having and keeping an out-of-quota child—this is a question I can answer.

"She does know your age," I say, but then I must tell her that I know this not because I know her birth mother but because her birth mother, having given birth to her, has this information from that experience.

Hours later, the cereal is still on the table. *What do I do?* I wonder. *Glue it to something? Put it in a frame? Memorialize it somehow?* I imagine us setting a dinner plate for Rose's birth mother image each night.

"I ate her legs," she says, "and she's angry."

Okay, I think, *now I'm really wishing for the book-on-everything so I can look up good and right and perfect responses.*

"I think my birth mother remembers me," Rose says.

Again, I am silent, wordless.

"Do strangers know when I was born?" she asks.

"No," I say, "not unless we tell them."

"I never want to tell strangers anything. I don't even want to talk to strangers about my birth mother. If they ask, I'm gonna walk away."

I remember these words, almost verbatim, from Beth O'Malley's *My China Workbook,* a guide for children adopted from China. I'm glad Rose knows she can keep details about her life private.

I take a picture of my daughter with the birth mother cereal.

"Don't throw her away," she says.

I wipe the crumbs into my hand and carefully place them back into the box.

The next morning, as I grab my cereal, Rose says, "Don't eat my birth mother."

"I'm having cereal," I say. "Do you want to talk about your birth mother?"

But before she can reply, she loses interest and is involved in an activity in the living room.

This gives a whole new meaning to a birth mother brunch, I think as I chew.

This parenting job is never going to get boring, I realize. I am so grateful, though, for the invitations, for the words and feelings my daughter is willing to share, and that I was big enough to share my cereal.

—Christine White

The child's name in this story has been changed to protect her privacy.

Amanda's Seeds

I know little about my background. I feel like parts of me are missing, because I don't know where I come from or, at least, from where half of my heritage springs. I was adopted within a family, and only half my history is mine; the other half is silent.

Being adopted means being a stranger to yourself and to your family. They don't understand the emptiness you feel every time they go through family photos. The family is yours by choice, their choice, and not by blood. You have as much connection to the faces and stories in a history book as you do to the faces in the family album. They're interesting and familiar, but no matter how much time you spend looking and hoping, there is no connection. I am luckier than most; I see my face in a few of those tattered and faded pictures, the half of my heritage we seldom visit and for which we have no records.

Like a stranger in a new country, I learned the language and speak with a good accent. However, I don't think in that "second" language. I am always running up against entrenched customs and asking why. I can't just accept. I want answers. They don't understand the questions. I am a cuckoo in a barn swallow's nest, a changeling.

I was surprised when my mother showed me a letter written by her great-grandmother Amanda, the heritage that belongs to my brother and sisters. Their roots grew from those flowing lines of fading script. The letter was dated just after the turn of the century. Yellow and ragged with age, it was written to Amanda's children—all ten of them.

"You're the only one who would appreciate this," my mother said when she gave it to me. "You're a lot like Amanda."

Amanda wrote of how her father came to America from Europe to build a better life for his family. He continued his traditions, farming the rich soil of the Midwest. Among the staple crops of potatoes, carrots, beans, and corn, he planted fruits and vegetables familiar to generations of his people.

As Amanda described her life, the colors and smells of her father's fields sprang to life around me. She wrote about the Hungarian peppers her father grew, how they burned deliciously on her tongue when she sneaked a taste of their fiery liquor from the canning pot. Money was scarce, but Amanda explained there was always plenty to eat. She preserved each season's harvest in jars and in words.

In each sentence, she painted her life in brilliant hues of hard work and the satisfaction of planning for the future. She outlined her dreams in shades of acceptance. She could never afford more education than she received at the local school and regretted she didn't have enough talent to be a writer.

Brought up to be a farmer's wife, she bore strong sons and daughters to continue the farming tradition. And harbored the hope that one of her children would realize her ambitions and become a writer.

I was transported to her world. I walked beside her as she picked multihued produce to eat and to preserve for the long cold winters when the fields were blanketed in snow. We gathered eggs still warm from the nests. We milked the cows; aiming the white streams into shining aluminum pails, I saw the milk froth and steam in the cold morning air. I understood the yearning to capture life in all its hardships and bounty, just as Amanda had when she chronicled her life. Through her descriptions of her garden, she helped her children to see the life she had lived and shared with them her hopes and dreams.

When I finished reading Amanda's letter, I called my mother and asked her to tell me more about her great-grandmother. She told me that Amanda had written to each and every one of her children religiously, offering them glimpses of the world she knew and the world she was coming to understand as her children moved away from the farm and on to other lives. In each letter, Amanda sowed the seeds of the past, tended the fruits of the present, and harvested her hopes for the future. Every letter was full of the life that flourished in her garden.

I copied Amanda's words onto my computer and marveled at what she had created in plain words and simple sentences. Her writing was never published, but there is no doubt she was a writer. Her gift was as beautiful and as rich as the vegetables she preserved like seeds in her letters.

Amanda's children never wrote more than occasional letters to their mother, each other, and their children. None of them or their children realized their mother's dream. Amanda's blood does not flow through my veins, but her dreams are mine. We are related, not by blood but through the writing that I have tended and planted with the seeds of the past—Amanda's seeds. She is my connection. I am heir to her dream.

—J.M. Cornwell

Near Brazigovo

On an early day in March, Stephen and Maggie stand by their hired car at the cross of two rough paved roads outside Brazigovo, in the heart of Bulgaria, people say. The newly plowed fields, orchards puffed with apple blossoms, rolling hills, and pale blue sky look like Ohio but feel like the end of the world to Maggie. They are waiting for the lawyer, Plamin, who is late. At home, they were told he would find them a child, file the adoption papers, and get their final decree; they're in good hands with Plamin. So last week's news made them leap: He had three healthy orphan toddlers with all of their documents.

"Perhaps it's a good sign that Plamin's late," Maggie offers.

Their translator, Sylvia, nods. Guidebooks had warned that the simplest gestures may deceive here. A nod means *no* in Bulgaria; a shake of the head *yes.* Stephen's eyes say, *never mind, let it go.*

Maggie can't. "What do you mean?" Silence. "Sylvia?"

"Nothing. I'm Bulgarian; I see bad signs." Sylvia snaps open a newspaper as if to say, *Waiting is your task now.*

Stephen takes out a puzzle with numbered tiles in a plastic frame he bought at the airport in Sofia. His fingers blur, sliding tiles to build elaborate sequences that he assigns himself. Because it calms him and Maggie needs his calm, she ignores the plastic *click-click-click* and tries to focus on the green-brown hills and the looping road that brought them here.

Two years ago, a noted gynecologist rapidly sketched her uterus on monogrammed notepaper, noting her organ's various defects, inelasticity, and the aging of her eggs. "You need help," he said, "before you miss the boat." So the assault began on Maggie's body. A nurse taught Stephen how to give her hormones, many needles every month. They had schedules for sex and sonograms to track the eggs—never more than two—down her tubes. "Younger women make six fresh eggs with a dose this size," the doctor chided. None of hers took hold, defective from the start or rejected by a "hostile" uterus. Perhaps both, the doctor suggested.

Her periods kept coming. Each month, Maggie fell deeper into depression, hormone-enhanced. She cried at night and dreamed of drowning in a hostile uterus. They worked hopelessly in bed and ate in silence. One morning Stephen threw down his fork and cried, "Enough! We can't go on with you like this." Maggie said, "You're right."

"Just finish up the cycle," the doctor urged, "this one could be it."

Could it be, or did he only want more cash?

"No thank you," Maggie said. "We've decided to adopt."

Everyone had advice. A friend told Stephen, "Call this number." "Sure, I'll get you a baby," a man responded, naming extraordinary sums to be paid to his "associates." Stephen thanked him and hung up. So their research began: Web sites, books, articles, workshops, endless calls to friends of friends.

"How about a handicapped child, blind or something?" suggested Maggie's friend Cindy, who had three healthy children. "If you'll take one like that, you go to the head of the list."

"What about multiple handicaps? Do I get a free wheelchair?" Maggie snapped.

It was a maze. One group needed notarized proof that both parents were baptized in the appropriate church. Healthy blond Russians came at staggering costs. A friend suggested open adoption, shared parenting with the birth mother. "I'm sorry," said Maggie, "I don't think we want to share."

In adoptive parents' support groups, they met Asian and Latin American children, then delicate, olive-skinned toddlers from Bulgaria with sudden luminous smiles. A Ukrainian aunt encouraged them: "The Slavic soul, the great Slavic heart." Bulgaria took root. They began collecting documents.

"No black market," Stephen warned the group leader. "No televisions." They'd heard of a couple bargaining a wide-screen color television for a newborn. When the birth mother signed a contract and then wanted more, their lawyer's men "dealt with her."

"No black market," the leader repeated. "But then you will need to be flexible about age."

They understood "flexible" and said a healthy toddler would be fine.

A black car approaches. "Maggie, that could be him," Stephen says and drops the puzzle into his pocket. Sylvia squints at the car, checks her watch, and shakes her head; yes, it's Plamin. He is tall, slouching, and slack-mouthed, wearing a leather jacket and scuffed pointed shoes. When Maggie and Stephen say in carefully memorized Bulgarian, "Hello, it is a pleasure to meet you," he looks past them.

Sylvia asks about the toddlers. Plamin nods *no*, not available.

"Why not?" Sylvia must be asking. He shrugs. Steven and Maggie grasp the words "no documents."

"But they had documents last week," Maggie insists. Sylvia translates.

Plamin doesn't answer. In the tilt of his cigarette, Maggie knows these three children never existed, with or without documents. The Plamin who worked for other couples will not work for them. He kicks the gravel, muttering. Sylvia hesitates.

"What?" demands Stephen.

"He says, 'I don't know if you're interested, but there's an institute nearby in Brazigovo with older children.'"

"How much older?" Bulgarian words flash back and forth. They hear "six," "seven," "eight."

"We wanted younger," Maggie insists. "He promised."

I'm losing it, she realizes. Like a plastic toy, she's breaking up in little snaps. First, she'd given up the dream of birthing, then the dream of adopting an infant. It had taken weeks to make a toddler suffice, to mold this image to her dreams: small hot hands around her neck, a small child riding on her hip, running to her, asking "carry me," "read to me," "play with me." At seven or eight, baby fat and baby needs are long gone. Now, there are friends and school and separate tastes and "Why can't I?" and "You're not fair!" and "I hate you if I can't do that!" Would such a child cry at night for Mommy, having lived so long without? Or shout "Daddy's home!" when no daddy ever was? They'd be shoving such a child straight into school with no family time at all. They'd have the awkward age and adolescence almost right away. Maggie knew the risks of adopting "older children": abandonment and acculturation issues, risks of nonattachment, and unsuccessful adoptions "interrupted" months or years later, every party hurt.

Of course, a happy blended family could emerge, just like in glossy women's magazines. But what if loving never comes? A family hell with no divorce? Then won't people smugly say, "But you knew the risks with an older child"?

A voice inside Maggie says, *Stick to what you want—a toddler, at least.*

Another voice replies, *At least go see. You don't know where you'll find your child, for sure not on this road.*

They drive into Brazigovo. A rose arbor leads to a high white building. "The institute," says Sylvia. A soft, round woman with orange hair answers their knock, listens to Sylvia, says some words, then "*direktor,*" and leaves them at the door. Plamin is silent.

Finally, hard shoes ring on stone floors. The director is tall, square-faced, not unkind. He talks to Sylvia while regarding Maggie and Stephen from top to toe. Maggie understands that he must study them, but her hand finds Stephen's and closes tightly around it. The director says in English, "Okay, hello, come." He gives instructions to the orange-haired woman, then brings them to his office and sits them down in plastic chairs. No one speaks.

Sylvia points out etchings of fierce-eyed men: "Bulgarian heroes, they freed us from the Turks."

"But did they adopt?" Stephen mutters to Maggie.

Murmurs outside the door, and a child's light knock tightens Maggie's stomach like a drum. The door opens. An orange flash, urgent words, then a slender, fawn-like child is pushed into the room: sweatshirt, ripped pants, rippling nut-brown hair, dark bright eyes, and the softest skin. She hovers near the door, gripping a balding, naked doll, but her head is up.

"Anna," they hear and "*Amerikanski.*" The director points to Maggie and Stephen. The child, too, regards them top to toe but does not speak, in fact, lifts the doll to mask her face.

"She's shy," Sylvia announces, then says insistently to Anna what must be, "Go on, speak!"

What child could speak, put on display like this? Maggie lays a hand on Sylvia's and whispers, "Never mind, we wouldn't understand her, anyway."

Anna peeps around the doll's bald head, and her breaking smile, arcing up and out, catches Maggie unprepared. She has to look away. *Hold on, watch out,* Maggie tells herself. *Remember what you wanted.* Her eyes find Plamin, who is rounding his cigarette ash and watching her intently.

Any word seems wrong. In the long silence, Stephen takes the puzzle from his pocket and starts moving tiles, tilting the whole toward Anna, making the sequence 1–2–3. When she inches forward, he says, "*Tuka*"—"Here"—and drops the puzzle into her hand. Soon, nimble fingers line up 4, 5, 6. Stephen points out 7, 8, 9, all scrambled, and Anna's little sigh, her furrowed brow, and the steady clicking all make Maggie shiver.

"How old is she?" Stephen asks over the child's bowed head. They hear "seven," but glances say it could be more.

The director speaks to Sylvia, who translates, "He hopes you'll tour the institute."

Maggie's throat tightens. "Thank him," she manages, "but perhaps we'd better go."

Words pass back and forth. "Just a few minutes, to see the children's work?"

It seems ungracious to refuse. As they file into the hall, Anna passes close, and Maggie stiffens, lacking words for, *Please don't touch me, child; you're too old for us.*

Anna takes Maggie's hand and finds Stephen's, too, holding tightly, fragile as she is. They are losing their way, far from where they meant to be. Plamin, the director, Sylvia, their own troubled and buffeted hearts—who can guide them now?

Anna smiles at Plamin. That smile. Plamin looks blankly back, then catching Maggie's eye, twists a smile around his cigarette and touches Anna's curls, his fingers stained with nicotine. *Get your filthy hands away from her!* Maggie wants to shout, but doesn't, of course. This isn't her child. She has no rights to Anna. When Maggie turns away, Plamin drops his hand and drifts toward a window, apparently bored with the tour.

The director watches Maggie intently now and slows his walk, pausing at each neat, Spartan bedroom, showing them embroidery samples made by the older girls and a dining room that smells of cabbage. Maggie and Stephen say what seems expected. Everywhere, solemn heroes look down on them. When Sylvia prompts her, Anna gravely recites a poem about the heroes, blushing when everyone claps for her.

They leave soon after, quickly. The orange-haired woman whom Sylvia calls "Aunt Elena" holds Anna as they pass beneath the rose arbor.

At the car, Plamin speaks to Sylvia, who answers sharply. "Go on," he seems to say, "tell them!"

"What?" Maggie demands.

"He says," Sylvia glances at Plamin, who stares blandly back at her, "that a French couple is considering Anna. So, if you want her, you need to decide right now. And he needs his fee up front."

"What French couple?"

Plamin speaks. Sylvia hesitates, then says, "The director told him while Anna recited the poem."

"But you didn't hear this?" Maggie demands.

Sylvia hesitates and then nods no.

"I see," says Maggie. So it's the "other party" trick of used-car dealers and shady real estate agents: bait and switch, act now, pay up front. They've heard the stories in adoption groups: couples in faraway countries who deal with men they'd never buy a toaster from at home, who abandon all familiar principles and come home empty-handed, bitter, had. She feels Stephen's hand on the small of her back. Yes, she understands. They can't go on with Plamin, and if not with him, most likely not with Anna either. She'll join the others of their children never born, washed away in blood.

Maggie bites her tongue as Stephen says to Sylvia, "If the French couple wants Anna, of course we wish her well. Thank Plamin for his time. We won't be needing his services anymore."

As Plamin stamps out his cigarette in the broken asphalt, words like puzzle pieces from their phrase book come to Maggie: "France—is—very—beautiful," she announces in Bulgarian.

The rest goes quickly: some words between Sylvia and Plamin. No handshakes. Plamin disappears in a blur of dust.

"I thought he'd spit on you," Stephen tells her in the car. They laugh a little, a drop of sweet in a bitter day.

Mortified by her countryman, Sylvia finds a café and orders a thick soup she says brings "comfort of the heart." The warmth, at least, is good, but Maggie grips her bowl and can't stop crying. The waitress brings napkins rough as newsprint. Stephen holds her as they sit without speaking until the late afternoon chill makes them shiver.

"Find us another lawyer," Maggie announces suddenly.

"A good one," Stephen adds, "nothing like Plamin."

Sylvia nods and stammers, "I just translate."

So finding another attorney is their job now. They enter a Kafkaesque world of hallways, pushing Sylvia—try this, explain that—and finally succeed. The new lawyer is expensive, of course, impersonal and laconic, but is said to be honest. His secretary beats out documents on a clanging Cyrillic typewriter. He makes certain calls, and Plamin fades away, drawn, as they suspected, into darker, faster waters.

They visit institutes and see toddlers, two boys and three girls, who stare back at them with baby blankness. One is cross-eyed. This can be fixed, Sylvia assures them hastily. Yes, of course. Still, they feel disloyal and uneasy. In restaurants, they strain their ears for French. Between appointments, walking aimlessly in parks, they watch children shoot past on bicycles, clamber over statues, pull on their parents' sleeves, crowd around a puppet show, offer bread to a trained monkey, squealing when he touches them.

"What are you thinking about?" they ask each other. Anna, always Anna.

Finally, they tell the new lawyer, "Take us to Brazigovo." Take us now, to beat the phantom Frenchmen, to act before Plamin gets wind of them.

When Anna, told the Amerikanski have come back for her, bursts into the director's office, she spins in a circle of light splashed on the gleaming floor and cries to Sylvia, "I'm so happy." When she eagerly copies what will be her new last name and announces, "I'll learn their language right away," their cup runs over. When Maggie gives Anna a music box and "Swan Lake" tinkles from her hand, she gasps and shivers with delight. But when she dashes to show the box to Aunt Elena, who kisses Anna's little face, Maggie is instantly jealous. How long before she's doing this in her house, to her own daughter?

They take pictures and then show Anna how to frame and focus. "*Da, ris birim,*" she says impatiently. "Yes, I understand." In fact, when her pictures come back, they are perfect.

The lawyer wants to go. "Work to do," he announces roughly. "Nice pictures don't make adoptions happen."

They understand but beg him to explain to Anna: Judges and decrees take time; she must be patient.

"No problem," the lawyer assures them hurriedly, "the director explains all."

The pain of this second parting makes them gasp. In the lawyer's Mercedes, they listen silently as he explains the various ministries that must examine and approve their papers.

At home the wait begins. Family and friends are polite, surprised, and mildly judgmental. "That old? You couldn't find a baby?" At a party, Maggie hears: "You're so good to take her in." She grips her glass. Charity, social work, second-string to motherhood, isn't that the implication? Those without a working uterus have got to be our saints? Maggie shoves these thoughts like heavy furniture to the corner of her mind and considers schools, shots, language classes, clothes. How big will Anna be in three months, four, five?

Six months pass, then more. They learn the child was not eight but nine, ten by now.

"Perhaps it's a sign," Maggie's friend Claudia suggests carefully. "Perhaps it wasn't meant to be."

"No," Maggie insists, but on what evidence? Yet, how can they possibly stop? Superstitious, they can't utter this choice, even to each other. They must pretend success is certain, lengthy but inevitable. Certainty is their grappling hook to haul themselves up and over each new obstacle. In Bulgaria, documents are mysteriously lost, then found again. The government falls, reforms, blocks and then grudgingly reopens foreign adoptions. A two-line fax arrives: Their lawyer is emigrating. His partner will take the case, but this adds time. He trusts they will be patient.

Friends fall away, at least fall silent. It's hard keeping company with people so obsessed, who have only bad news and this news so numbingly complex. Meanwhile, stories come at them, shoved up by near strangers and a seeming conspiracy of the media: healthy babies easily obtained, one from a neighbor's sister. Imagine, so close to home! Questions asked or intimated: Why pick such a hard way; why keep pushing?

One of Maggie's colleagues says outright, "No offense, but of course she made like she wanted you. Wouldn't any child want out of an orphanage?"

"You just saw her, what, twice?" a near stranger who heard their story demands. "How do you know she's the one?"

"Strange, isn't it?" returns Stephen, staring the woman down.

Friends are more difficult. "Haven't you thought of making your own?" Francesco jokes at a picnic by his pool, and then is so embarrassed by Maggie's cataract of tears that he spills red wine on her shirt. "That was a dumb thing to say. I'm so sorry," he says over and over as they blot the stain with water "It's nothing to laugh about."

"No, the fact is, I'm losing all kinds of perspective. Let me take a swim. I'm wet already," Maggie announces and swims lap after lap as the party rattles on.

Naturally, their marriage tangles in the net. There's so little energy left for joy. They push on even here, dragging their lives behind them. They take vacations and endure holidays, but don't prepare a bedroom or study Bulgarian. If the un-nameable happens, they don't want words in a strange alphabet loose in their minds or dolls propped on a little bed. Even memories scald: Anna reciting poetry, breathless at the door, radiant with her music box, writing her name in Roman letters, waving them goodbye. When Maggie says, "Remember when—" Stephen pleads, "Don't, it doesn't help me."

Maggie cannot stop. Waking, working, falling fitfully to sleep, their imagined future as a family grows as sharp as their tiny past together. Then, on an ordinary day in May, their new lawyer faxes: He's expecting the final decree.

Maggie's dream becomes a movie now, with music and full effects.

Fade in: *Brazigovo. They pass under the rose arbor. Music anticipates joy. A door thrown open; Anna*

running out, crying: "They came back for me."
Strings soar to major key.

New scene: *That night in their hotel, they comfort Anna's racking tears, and she folds to them, big as she is, as they rock her to sleep. Next day: Learning English with games and rhymes; strolling through Sofia, she grips their hands as they slowly weave a life together.*

Fade out: *They board a plane for home, a family already.*

In late July, Stephen and Maggie's hired car pulls up to the institute in Brazigovo again. Fourteen months have elapsed. Their lawyer precedes them, carrying the decree. Their steps ring under the arbor, but no one runs to them. Approaching, they hear a muffled cry inside. When the door is opened, they see Elena comforting Anna, who has buried her face in Elena's pillow breasts. Anna is taller, with her curls pinned up. She will not look at them. They all stand awkwardly in the entry.

"I have documents for the director," the lawyer says. "You can start to know each other."

How? Maggie freezes, her knees locked, her arms stiff at her side. *This dress is wrong, I look too thin,* is all she's thinking. *I don't have breasts like Elena.*

The lawyer and director disappear. Elena gently pats a couch, urging Anna to sit, "Here, with Mama and Daddy." Anna clings to Elena's skirt, far away from them. When Stephen takes out his game with numbered tiles, she stares grimly at the floor.

"Never mind," says Stephen easily. He takes out another game, this one from a toy store. "I'll play Four-in-a-Row with Elena. It works like this," he explains in English and slow gestures. Elena's large face studies the disks. "*As ris birim*," she says quietly. "I understand."

Maggie, suddenly tired and lonely, wants to lean her own head on that soft breast. Stephen drops a red disk in a slot, then Elena drops a black. She explains the game coaxingly to Anna. "It's fun," she must be saying, "try." Anna won't try or even watch. After Elena wins, they sit in silence broken only by the distant rustle of lawyer's documents. The Bulgarian heroes stare, giving no help.

"Try the whistle," Stephen says.

When Maggie draws a purple lollipop from her bag, Anna's eyes light up. Encouraged, Maggie says in Bulgarian she learned on the plane, "Candy whistle. Blow!" Startled eyes turn to her. Maggie wonders, *Have I said something idiotic, threatening, obscene?* Anna shrinks, staring at the lollipop that seems to bloom in Maggie's hand. It has to work now. Maggie tears off the plastic, puts the lollipop to her mouth, blows a piercing note, and then mimes an eager licking. Even the heroes seem intrigued. "*Ti*," Maggie says. "For you." Anna takes it gingerly, never touching Maggie. "Go on," Elena must be saying, "blow." Anna does, first low, then a long, shrill blast. Now, at last, that heart-opening smile returns and the delicious rippling laugh from long ago, but the lovely face is turned to Elena.

The lawyer and director return. Anna's few clothes sit by the door in plastic bags. When she grasps that she is leaving now, with the Amerikanski and without Elena, Anna shrieks, grappling Elena. Maggie and Stephen feel like kidnappers.

"Did she think Elena was coming?" they ask the lawyer. "Didn't they explain?"

"Of course, a hundred times," the lawyer assures them. "Remember, she's leaving her only home."

Maggie remembers the other Anna who took their hands and aches for needing that one. *You're the grownup*, Maggie chides herself, *not the one who should be needing.*

The lawyer speaks brightly to Anna. The crying stops abruptly. "I promised you'd buy her ice cream in Sofia," he translates.

Anna lets herself be kissed by Elena and climbs into the car, where she sits staring straight ahead, hands clasped in her lap, apparently waiting for ice cream.

"Is there a message here?" Stephen murmurs. "Something we should get?"

On the long drive to Sofia that Maggie has imagined a hundred thousand times but never grim like this, Anna does learn to play Four-in-a-Row but will not answer any question they have the lawyer put to her and has none at all for them. *At least she's playing*, Maggie tells herself. *Tonight in the hotel with the teddy bear they've brought her, their family will begin. There's so much of love that needs no words.*

In the hotel, Anna goes immediately to sleep, turned away from them. They'll have at least a week in this country until the visa comes, they remind themselves. Surely, she'll get used to them and slowly grow to love them. Isn't that how adoption stories go?

The next day it's clear that nothing in the months of waiting for this child was as piercingly hard and humiliating as having her. The zoo raises a flicker of interest when a black bear stands to catch food that Anna throws at him; she imitates the bear in their hotel room, and they laugh. They learn "*metchko*" for bear and "*sladaled*" for ice cream, which Anna always wants. They learn words for bananas, chips, comic books, various kinds of clothes, and Barbie dolls. Anna seems to see them as a bank. They don't mind at first; she needs so many things, and it's good to see her even briefly happy, although rarely because of them, if anything, despite them.

They can't touch her, especially Stephen. "*Ti, neh,*"—"You, no"—she says if he comes close. And "*Neh, pussh!*" "No, leave me alone."

"Show an active interest in your child's birth culture," all adoption books suggest. "Buying local handicrafts for your home is an excellent way of bonding." Anna prefers German news broadcasts, even farm reports, to bonding time with them.

She won't learn English or even try. "Water," Maggie coaxes, holding the child's hand under the hotel faucet. "*Ni ris birim,*" Anna insists. "I don't understand."

"What's to understand?" Maggie asks aloud. "Helen Keller understood."

At night, Maggie imitates frogs. Anna listens briefly, then turns away to sleep. Day by day, their patience wanes. On buses, Anna sits as far away as possible, holding animated conversations with strangers, as if to say, "See, I like other people very well." Family and friends are waiting for their calls, but what can they say? Perhaps we made a terrible mistake?

In a park outside the consulate, Anna points eagerly to an ice cream vendor. When they say no, three *sladaled* in a morning is plenty, she throws herself screaming on the ground. People stare and wonder, no doubt, *Who are those foreigners with a Bulgarian child who doesn't want them?* Picking Anna up and hauling her, kicking, to a bench, Stephen hurts his back. "If they arrest us, fine," he mutters. "The police can deal with her."

"*Sladaled sega?*" Anna demands when Stephen finally stands erect. "Ice cream now?"

"Remember how your child must feel," the books all say. What about our feelings, Maggie wants to ask. Who will comfort us?

Anna *does* like restaurants. She likes menus, waiters, and food that isn't cabbage. On the fifth night, they find a Chinese restaurant. She's delighted with chopsticks and lets Maggie show her how to use them. They give her coins to stack in piles. Stephen rests his hand near her plate until Anna takes the bait. She grasps his thumb with chopsticks and lifts it in the air, laughing, that edible, heart-stopping laugh. They play until the eggrolls come. Relaxed and hopeful, Maggie and Stephen finish a bottle of wine. Anna wants ice cream, then another. They let her. Really, why not indulge her? When Anna doesn't want the waiter's tip left on the table and extravagantly mimes a thief pouncing on their change, Stephen takes Anna to find the waiter and lets her give the tip.

They're so hopeful, but walking to the bus, it's *"Neh, pussh!"* again when they try to take her hand. She won't wait at the corner and runs past the bus stop. Stephen has to drag her back. *"Neh, pussh!"* is even harder after wine. The books warned of this as well: The child comes close and then turns away, fearful to be hurt again. But the books don't say how to get her on the bus with you.

The last bus that night comes hissing and groaning down on them. When the doors creak open, Anna bolts away. An unspoken question blooms between them: *Suppose we just get on, just us? What stops them? Honor? Pride? Documents? Hope?* They'll never know. At the last instant, Maggie shouts in English, "Wait!"—and the driver seems to understand. They grab Anna, one at each arm, and haul her to the bus. She kicks and flails, screaming *"Pussh! Pussh!"* and bracing herself at the door.

The driver speaks sharply. "On or off," no doubt he's saying. "I want to go home."

"Pussh yourself! Get on the damn bus!" snaps Stephen so sharply that the screaming stops. He drags Anna through the door, arms pinned down like a collapsed umbrella. *"Tuka!"* he orders, "Here!"—

pointing at four empty seats in the back, two pairs facing each other. When Anna doesn't move, he picks her up and drops her in the aisle seat. "I said *tuka! Ris birim?*" "Understand?" Anna moves to the window seat, glaring out. Stephen and Maggie sit down heavily across from her. Passengers stare. So what?

At the next stop, two squat countrywomen clamber on the bus, each with bulging sacks of produce. Now the only empty seat is next to Anna. The bigger woman speaks roughly: something-something "little girl," then waves toward the aisle, where apparently Anna should stand and let her elders sit. Anna's face is rigid, still glaring out the window. She doesn't budge.

When the bus groans and swerves, the woman lurches into Stephen and barks again at Anna. There is no way they can explain, "This child who doesn't look or act like ours is ours. Leave her alone." Stephen gestures to the woman, "Here, take our seats." He and Maggie start to rise, but a heavy hand keeps him down. Abruptly, Anna stands, slides past them, and disappears into the rocking crowd. Instantly, the women squeeze into the two now-empty seats.

Wedged in place, Maggie cranes her neck to look for Anna. There she is, right behind the countrywomen, frowning at their angry muttering as they browse through sacks of vegetables. Anna's eyes swing toward Maggie's, catch and draw them back to the lowing women. Anna puffs her cheeks and slides two forefingers up her face and out through soft brown curls, now they're horns. From her rounded mouth the faintest "moo" emerges. Maggie tries to frown—"don't do that"—but it's funny, really. Maggie hides her mouth. The two horns wiggle, then vanish when an old man glances from his book to Anna.

The bus stops again; late workers, teenaged couples, and noisy drunks jostle on and off. Where's Anna? Pushed out? No, she's tapping Stephen's elbow, then calmly pushing past him, bumping the women's knees and pushing aside the vegetables. One of them snaps what must be, "Hey, kid! What's going on?" Anna doesn't answer, just sits down hard on Maggie's lap. She ignores a second question, too, merely thrusts her hand in Stephen's pocket, pulls out his game of Four-in-a-Row, and with a smirk at the staring women, carefully divides the colored disks.

When the bus tilts and groans at a hard curve, Maggie wraps her arms around the little waist, and the child's weight melts against her chest. The whole jouncing way back to the hotel, they sit like this.

"*Neh, pussh,*" says Stephen once when Anna tries to sneak a disk. "Get your cotton-picking fingers out of there!"

"Cotton-picking," Anna repeats carefully, "cotton-picking fingers."

—*Pamela Schoenewaldt*

The names and some personal details of the people in this story have been changed to protect their privacy.

A version of this story was first published under the title "Near Brazigovo" in Iron Horse Literary Review, Fall 2000.

Special Sisters

"This is my cousin," my thirteen-year-old sister, Shelly, announced to the bus driver, pointing at me as we boarded the city bus to go to our tap class.

Her cousin? I stared at my older sister, surprised into silence, unusual for my chatty, ten-year-old self. Okay, in a way she was right. I was my parents' biological child, born three years after Shelly's adoption, while Shelly's birth father was my father's brother, Uncle Walt. But legally, and in every other way except the birth thing, we were sisters. She was just weird telling the bus driver we were cousins, like she wanted to broadcast it to the whole world.

"What did you say that for?" I demanded as we took a double seat near the front of the bus. "I'm your sister and you know it." I punched her in the arm.

"You're my cousin and you know it. My real father wants me to go live with him, if you want to know. I have two sisters and a brother there." Shelly sounded defiant, but something in her eyes didn't match her tone of voice.

I knew Shelly had seen Uncle Walt when we all went to Arizona for summer vacation. Since he'd divorced Shelly's mother and remarried, much more happily I'd heard, maybe he did want her back.

She was his only child, given up for adoption. But he'd asked my parents to take her, and he shouldn't be able to change his mind now.

My stomach did a hop and a jump. Would Shelly really leave and go live with him? Was I that unimportant to her?

Sure, we fought like two scrappy terriers sometimes, arguing over who left the ironing board up, who stole whose charm bracelet, who forgot to feed the goldfish. But we also shared any clothes that would fit us both, from puffy crinolines to cap-sleeved blouses. We threw pairs of rolled-up socks between our twin beds at night and were frequent co-conspirators on plans to whip through our Saturday chores in time to go with neighbors to the beach. Shelly was a part of our family as much as I was. We loved each other. Didn't we?

"Nobody will miss me, anyway," Shelly said. Tears sparkled in her eyes. "They like you better. My father said so. That's why I should live with him."

"That's crazy," I said "Mom and Daddy brag a lot more about you than they do me. Just ask them."

"I'm not saying a word to them about this, and neither are you," Shelly hissed. "You're too dumb to understand anything."

Crushed into silence, I slouched deeper into the broad bus seat. A big lady across the aisle caught my eye and smiled. Did she think this was some typical fight between sisters? Shelly had never said shut up to me. No one spoke those words in our home. And she'd never said I was dumb. We sat in smoldering silence until we reached dance class.

Brush-tap, brush-tap, brush-tap, our tap dance instructor coached us. I tried to concentrate on the warm-up exercise, but all I could think of was Shelly. *Why does she hate me all of a sudden?*

It seemed like after that conversation on the bus I couldn't do anything right, from picking out a pair of shoes to dusting the living room furniture . . . at least according to Shelly, whom I had worshipped my entire life and accepted as the ultimate authority on all things.

I fought back like a wounded animal in whatever way I could. I told her she was mean and selfish and tattled on her for everything she did that might make our parents cross. Our sibling rivalry burned with the intensity of a pile of dry timber torched on a windy afternoon.

We still had good times, though.

"You can borrow my blue wool skirt and white sweater set," Shelly said one afternoon as she helped me get ready for an after-school dance. "The color is perfect on you."

Another time we took our allowance and went together to Ralph's grocery store to buy movie magazines and to tape pictures of our current heartthrobs on our bedroom wall.

But those occasions grew increasingly rare. Shelly asked for her own bedroom, and I was banished to the guest room upstairs. She wouldn't play board games with me anymore on the family room table or do gymnastics on our front lawn. "Go away. Quit following me," she would command if her friends were around.

I got madder and madder, more and more hurt. One day, a year or so after the scene on the bus, when she'd spent more than her usual hour beautifying herself in our shared bathroom, I banged on the door. "Shelly, I want in," I demanded.

"Go away," she snarled. "I'm not finished."

"Don't be such a brat. I have to get ready for a birthday party."

"Well, tough," she said. "I'll open the door when I'm good and ready."

In my rage, I kicked the bathroom door as hard as I could. "Ouch," I screamed, hopping into the living room, where I collapsed on the couch, crying.

I don't remember if I went to the birthday party. I do remember that I broke my big toe and walked with crutches for weeks. My broken toe healed, but the tension between us didn't. As far as I know, Shelly's birth father never pursued his invitation for Shelly to go live with him. Shelly had commanded my silence about that encounter, and for some reason, I honored her wish. I doubt there were any family conversations that would have explained our behavior to our parents. They must have wondered why we were both so wracked with insecurities, stumbling and slinking through adolescence, arguing every step of the way.

With increasing frequency, Mother would sit at the kitchen table, her head in her hands. "Oh, girls, stop bickering," she would moan. "You're giving me a migraine." My father often escaped our endless arguing by gardening or going on long walks after his day at work.

Shelly married when she was eighteen, moved into an apartment with her husband not far from my parents in Southern California, and started a family. I went off to college, then married and moved to Oregon.

From a geographic and an emotional distance, I watched Shelly grow into an amazingly generous, caring person. Somehow, she took all her hurt and turned it into love. She and her husband took care of my parents in a hundred ways. Her birth parents and siblings became a second family as she reached out to all of them, visiting her brother and two sisters, taking flowers to her mother in a nursing home, and visiting her father whenever she could. She maintained an extensive network of good friends as well. She included me in that circle of family and friends, occasionally phoning or emailing, and never forgetting me on my birthday or Christmas.

I reciprocated with cards, gifts, and e-mails. Still, I felt a wide abyss separating us. The ten-year-old in me who had been so hurt and betrayed on the bus that day didn't quite trust her love. *We aren't close because we live more than a thousand miles apart and have very different interests,* I'd tell myself. The deeper truth was that I felt she kept in touch with a staggeringly long list of people and I was just one of them, not someone truly special to her.

We did connect on several important occasions. We clung to each other as we faced our mother's death. Shelly and her husband and daughter made a two-day drive to my wedding when I remarried. We talked more often of our shared childhood and about the rough spots for us growing up. But I kept a protective shield around my heart.

Then, when my husband and I and another couple were planning a hiking trip near the town where Shelly and her husband lived, I called to see if we could visit.

"Come to dinner and bring your friends," she said immediately.

A few weeks later, she led the four of us into her kitchen, where she had prepared a buffet line. I was stunned at the feast before me: a green salad and coleslaw; a platter of golden brown chicken and one of juicy ribs; baked potatoes with butter, sour cream, and chives; a mounded bowl of saffron rice; fresh wheat rolls and white rolls; steaming corn on the cob.

"Save room for dessert," Shelly said as she handed us each a plate.

"Who else is coming?" I asked, amazed at the size of the banquet.

"Just you," she said.

"Oh, Shelly," I murmured, and tears started to fill my eyes. My sister lived a busy life and operated on a slim budget. Yet, she had taken the time and spent what must have been her grocery budget for the month to do all this for me. I was dazed with happiness.

"She really cares about you," my husband whispered as we stacked our plates with food.

I finally saw it. I threw my arms around Shelly. "I feel so special," I said, kissing her cheek.

"You are special," she said and squeezed me tight before releasing me. "You're my sister."

—*Samantha Ducloux Waltz*

Some names in this story have been changed to protect the privacy of those individuals.

Scenes from the Broken Road

"Where could they be?"

Ignoring the giggling from the closet, I look in all the silly places: under the desk, under the books, in the trash can. Finally, at the prompting of the other Sunday school kids, I open the closet door, and two little boys look up at me, grinning and giggling. Their faces are heaven lit.

Later, I laugh when I tell one of my Sunday school kids' parents that, when my husband and I are ready to have children, I want theirs.

I'm cradling the cat in my arms. She's tiny, like a human baby. I pet her face and look down at her, wondering what it would be like to hold my own baby in my arms. When nobody can hear me, I call her my baby girl.

I can't stand to hold my friend's baby this morning. Just looking at her fills me with longing and sorrow and anger and resentment. It's the anger and resentment that make me cry, because it was my own choice not to have children when my husband and I were young. Now I feel old, like my chance at motherhood is gone.

We're eating dinner together at Denny's: my husband, his mom, our niece, and me. Our niece asks something, and I almost say, "Ask your father"—only I'm referring to my husband, not our niece's father. I stop eating, forkful of omelet halfway to my mouth, and wonder how it would feel to actually say it.

I'm blowing bubbles, waiting for the little monsters' parents to come pick them up. I enjoy volunteering in the church nursery, but ten kids all under the age of three are a handful. After two hours, I'm ready for their parents to take them home.

Then I notice Zack. He's making little sighing noises, bouncing up on his toes, reaching out for his turn to pop the bubbles. It's the sweetest sound I've ever heard, and all my negativity bursts like little bubbles on his tiny hands.

A church member stops me in the hall to tell me what a joy it is to have my daughter in her Sunday school class. My heart is in my throat when I tell her she must have mistaken me for somebody else. On any other day, I would have handled it better, but today my heart is breaking over how long it's taking just to get our home study finished and approved.

I check out every book in the library system about a particular disorder, because we've been approached about adopting twin girls diagnosed with it. After my research, I feel confident about our ability to parent them, and we tell our social worker yes. Every time I pass the spare bedroom and see the empty twin beds, I imagine the girls sleeping in them.

I stop keeping track of how many kids we've asked about and said yes to, because my heart is broken from so much silence. Adoption is a black hole. We send our home study out again and again but rarely hear anything back. When we do, it's usually not good—like when the twins' foster parents changed their minds and decided to adopt the girls after all.

We finally meet her, The One, only she's not allowed to know we want to adopt her. I want to take her in my arms and hold her the first time I see her, but I'm still a stranger. I feel like a silly school-girl on a first date: trying to stay near her, wishing I could hold her hand, wanting to hug her but afraid of being too forward.

Afterward, my husband tells me he knew she was meant to be our daughter at first sight. I agree.

On our way back to her foster home, we sing songs from *The Sound of Music*. She leans forward from the back seat and declares, "We make a good team." I wonder if she knows.

She's sitting in my husband's lap. "I don't want to leave," she tells him.

My heart leaps into my throat.

"It's not our decision right now," he says.

I want to tell her that I never want her to leave. The house is so empty when she's not here.

A week after she finally moves home, I drive to her former foster home to pick up some of her things. For a moment, I feel like I'm picking her up again, expecting to see her when I walk through their front door. I have to remind myself that she doesn't live there anymore. I smile and enjoy the thought that we won't ever have to take her back again.

As I dry my hair in the morning, I suddenly see her in the mirror. She picks up the cat and sits on the bed to pet it. I forget she's there and don't notice her getting up and disappearing again. Then she's behind me, saying "Boo!" as loudly as she can, and I'm yelling "Holy moly!" and laughing at the same time.

I'm in bed, trying to fall asleep. I hear my daughter come into the bedroom, as she often does when I'm so tired that I go to bed before her. I keep my eyes closed, like I usually do when she thinks I'm sleeping. But this time I wait until she gets right next to me, then I say "Boo!" instead of letting her kiss my forehead and whisper "goodnight" to me.

I'm dropping her off for school. It's been a rough morning, and we've both been crying. She closes the door without saying "goodbye" or "have a nice day" or "I love you." She looks at me through the window. I try to keep my face neutral, but she must see the hurt in my eyes. She opens the door again and leans in for a goodbye kiss anyway.

The day before Mother's Day, she puts her arms around me and tells me, "I love you so much." I kiss her forehead when she looks up at me and says, "Happy Mother's Day Eve."

I thank her and tell her I love her.

She says, "I love you too."

I tell her, "I love you three."

She says, "I always love you one more than you love me."

It's my first Mother's Day, and I'm lying on the couch, curled up in a comforter, trying to take a nap. She's sitting nearly on my lap, trying to convince me to play a game with her instead. I try to convince her that it's my day to do whatever I want. We're both giggling.

I tell her, "You were supposed to bring me breakfast in bed," and "I had to cut my own flowers!"

But she doesn't want to hear it and puts her hand over my mouth, so it comes out more like, "Oo wa thupotht oo mming me mmekfeth in med," and "I a oo cu muh oooh thowah!"

We're driving up Liberty Road. We could be going to school or church or the store; it doesn't matter. The CD is playing one of our favorite songs, "Bless the Broken Road," by Rascal Flatts. We sing along. We're both off-key and out of tune; that doesn't matter, either.

I wonder if she knows that, for me, this song is about her . . . that God blessed the broken road to my long-lost dream of motherhood and led me straight to her.

—Kim Gonzalez

Yuanjun's Home

Shanghai is a city of breathless beauty. It straddles the winding Huangpu River, a tributary of the mighty Yangtze. The air is heavy with moisture and heat. Day and night, the sidewalks and streets are crowded and noisy. Beautiful women in silk *qí páo* dresses glide past tired beggars; lines of schoolchildren march through throngs of shouting businessmen. In this city of 13 million people, we are here to meet one special citizen. We have arrived from Washington State, and we feel as though we have been traveling toward this day in Shanghai for an eternity, to meet our new son, Xu Yuanjun.

My husband Mark and I have adopted from China twice before. Each time, we have been awed by the beauty of the country and the kindness of its citizens. Children are everywhere in the People's Republic of China. Most families have only one child each, and we see how proudly they are held, how tenderly they are guarded. We later learn that Yuanjun's parents cared for him lovingly, but they were too poor to keep him. At seven years of age, Yuanjun has been waiting to be adopted since age three.

The Shanghai Children's Welfare Institute is a tall, somber building in the heart of Shanghai. A small courtyard graces its entrance. We are both excited and apprehensive to meet Yuanjun at last. Like a talisman, Mark clutches our only picture of our new son. If we are this anxious, how must Yuanjun be feeling? We had first seen Yuanjun's face in a collage of waiting children sent out by our adoption agency. Mark had fallen in love with Yuanjun after seeing this small picture. In the photo, Yuanjun stares gravely at the photographer, but his black eyes reveal a sweetness and a longing that captured our hearts.

Yuanjun is finally ushered into the meeting room. I am so excited I can barely breathe. Our new son meets us with shy glances and a nervous smile. I speak haltingly in my stilted Mandarin. *"Hen gaoxing renshi ni. Ni hao,"* I tell him gently. "I am very happy to meet you. How are you?"

Yuanjun answers softly, *"Hao ba, xiexie. Nin hao, nin shi mama? Nin shi fuqin? Zhaopian ma? Jiu na xie?"*

"Fine, thank you. You are the mother, the father from the photographs?"

He is clutching the small photo album we sent to him a few months ago—pictures of his new family and of the small farm in America he will come to call home. We speak carefully to each other, and a tenuous thread forms.

First, Yuanjun must show us his room at the orphanage, his home for the past several years, his family of caretakers, and the friends he will leave behind. Yuanjun watches us solemnly for a moment before he extends his hand to me. I am honored and follow him to the winding stairway that leads up to his floor. Beaming at our new son, Mark walks close behind. Yuanjun has bilateral clubfeet, and so we move slowly up the stairs, resting every few steps. Eight flights take a long time to climb when your legs don't work well.

At last, we reach our destination and Yuanjun holds open the door politely. His face is ruddy from exertion, and I think in wonder, he climbs those eight flights of stairs several times each day.

Yuanjun introduces me to his caretaker, Abu, and I struggle again with my limited Mandarin. "I am pleased to meet you. So grateful to you . . ." What words to pick, to thank her for our son's care? She has protected, cuddled, and loved him for all of his years in the orphanage; how bravely she smiles through her tears.

The large room is filled with boys of all ages. Beds are lined up neatly with colorful quilts rolled tightly against the south wall. All activity stops as children gather around us. Some look envious of Yuanjun and some seem frightened. We have brought small presents, and the gray-haired Abu distributes them carefully amongst the boys. "*Xie, xie,*" the children tell us gravely as they disperse to study their small treats. Only Yuanjun's special friends gather around him—one already crying.

"*Bu ku, wo pengyou,*" our new son comforts him. "Don't cry, my friend."

Then, it is time to leave. Yuanjun wipes his face angrily, but the weeping will not stop. His Abu holds him for a moment, ignoring her own tears. She murmurs softly while we fight back our own sorrow for their pain. Our son has endured so many partings already. He came to the orphanage at three years of age. Yuanjun's parents could not care for him because of his serious orthopedic problems and because they had a second son. Their only hope was for him to be adopted and have the surgery he needed. So much grief.

In the hotel later, Yuanjun gazes once more at the small photo album. He is not looking at the faces of his new family but at the wondrous sight of his future home. Having lived in an anonymous building of 300 children, the snapshot of our sprawling farmhouse seems to overwhelm him. He traces the pictures again, his stubby fingers resting on the bright red door, the large windows, and the chaotic beds of flowers.

Feeling my gaze, he looks up and offers an explanation. *"Wo-de jiali? Zhen piaoliang."* "My home? So beautiful."

On the long flight home, sad and again close to tears, Yuanjun stares at the photos again. New parents, new siblings, new relationships—all are so fraught with peril for a frightened seven-year-old. But this house, this farm—Yuanjun falls in love with those from the moment we pulled up at the gate.

Our seven other children tumble out the front door, and we are engulfed for several minutes. Yuanjun manages to tolerate this with good grace, but already his attention has been drawn to the two-story farmhouse, before him at last. Two of Yuanjun's new brothers begin to tug him up the steps to the front porch. They are babbling excitedly in English, and a brief look of panic crosses Yuanjun's face. "It's all right," I call to him in Mandarin. "You can go with them; we're coming, too."

But still, he must move slowly. He touches the red door reverently before entering. John and Shen Bo lead him up the stairs to their shared bedroom. "This is your bed, your dresser!" they say. Yuanjun does not understand their English but grasps their meaning. By the time we join them, he is sitting cross-legged on his bed, a look of pure joy on his face. He smoothes the new yellow comforter and risks a bold move: he hugs the two teddy bears sitting on his new pillows.

Later, he is stunned to find new, neatly folded clothes in the pine dresser next to his bed and a shiny collection of toy cars. "*Zhe shi wo-de ma?*" "For me?" he asks. "All this is for me?"

He laughs out loud when he sees the kitchen. A pantry full of strange food, an icebox crammed with enticing mysteries. All for one family! Our first meal together at the table is too exciting for him. He can manage only a few bites as he contemplates each of us in turn. Sitting at the long birch table, he suddenly notices the distant mountains through the tall windows: snow on the Cascades and Mount Baker to the north, rising high above them all. Worn out by such wonders, his eyes drift shut, his head slides toward the table. Before his glossy black hair can land in his plate, my husband whisks him off to bed, to his own beautiful bed.

Each day is a discovery for Yuanjun. Such courage it takes, to simply wake up and step into the morning, so many discoveries. Brothers and sisters, he can understand, having just come from a place of 300 such "siblings." But two parents, a mother and a father—we are a gift he opens slowly, cautiously. It must be with relief, then, that he can enjoy the uncomplicated delight of his new home, a present he can tear into with joy. And he does. He explores all of the bedrooms, the old upright piano in the living room, the thrill of television and American cartoons. He runs his fingers over the rows of books in the bookcases and touches the candles in the dining room. He stretches himself out on the deep red Oriental rug. So much space!

Yuanjun inspects the three bathrooms. Three of them for only ten people; can you imagine? Mark gives him a bubble bath in the old claw-footed tub. Shen Bo wants to join him in the bath, but Yuanjun is firm. For once in his life, Yuanjun will take a bath alone, no crowding, no sharing; such luxury, such a large grin!

And then outside to the farm itself! Our small farm feeds our family, with some left over to sell to neighbors and friends. Yuanjun laughs in disbelief when I show him the orchard filled with blooming apple trees. Apples (*pin guo*) from trees? Ridiculous!

For this city boy, apples came from market stalls and require much haggling. Live chickens (*ji*) scare him. He has only seen them hanging and already dead, to be purchased and eaten. He gasps with pleasure when he sees the many eggs (*jidan*) in the coop's nests.

In China, he occasionally had a delicious treat—a hard-boiled egg—and loved it. Before I can stop him, he grabs an egg from the straw nests. Imagine his look of shock when the raw egg breaks and dribbles down his shirt!

The cows take his breath away. Though the sweet-faced Jerseys regard him calmly, Yuanjun slips his hand into mine and closes his eyes tightly. When he looks again, though, they are still there, breathing their warm alfalfa smell over us and chewing their cud sedately. Such large animals! Such a place! At least the cows are gentle and move slowly. The noisy, rambunctious pigs (*zhu*), on the other hand, are best viewed from a safe distance.

Yuanjun watches as Brendan milks Lily. As the steaming milk fills the large pails, Yuanjun shakes his head incredulously. Milk from a cow! It will be several weeks before he agrees to drink milk again.

His new sisters—Sara, Emma Rose, and Chengming—drag him across the green pastures. Shanghai has many lovely parks, but somehow Yuanjun has never seen grass. Sara takes off his shoes, and Yuanjun giggles when the clover and timothy grass tickle his feet but balks at walking barefoot across it. His misshapen feet beneath him, he runs his hands over the long soft blades of grass and then bends to smell the rich earth.

"Ah, another farmer," Mark says proudly. Though Mark is a physician, as I am, he takes much pride in our farm and the labor needed to tend it. Now riding high on Mark's shoulders, Yuanjun leans low and plants a soft kiss on my upraised hand. Shen Bo jealously grabs my other hand. Happily in custody, I let my two sons pull me home.

Yuanjun, my stouthearted boy, undergoes surgery only three months after arriving in this country. His crooked feet are getting worse, and his doctors fear he will suffer irreparable damage to his ankle and knee joints. We cannot put off treatment any longer if we hope to give him straight limbs to run on.

Before we leave for the hospital, he kisses each of his siblings goodbye. Finally, he enters his room and gazes at it hungrily. He rearranges the bright yellow quilt on his bed, lines up his shiny Matchbox cars, and kneels down to pray. He is familiar with Buddhism and chants softly in Mandarin. It is a moment of solemnity that is made humorous by his brothers, Shen Bo and John, joining him in supplication. Shen Bo ruins the quiet scene by completing a forward somersault from his position of genuflection.

Four-year-old Shen Bo is a person of transcendent exuberance. He simply cannot resist tormenting his many older siblings. He further complicates matters by announcing to Yuanjun, "I get to have all your cars when you're at the hospital!"

Yuanjun howls in anger and bellows at his baby brother. "Bad boy, Shen Bo! No you touch my bed, my toys when I am at doctor!"

With a mischievous grin, Shen Bo hops over to Yuanjun's bed. He places his little hand on Yuanjun's soft comforter and laughs. "Touch. Touch, touch, touch!" Spinning away from Yuanjun, he runs out the door, chortling.

Yuanjun lumbers after him. "You no my friend!" he calls to Shen Bo.

John attempts to salvage the moment. "It's okay, Yuanjun. He isn't your friend; he's your brother."

In the hospital, Yuanjun waits impatiently for his surgeon. The hospital staff has encouraged us to bring in a special "lovey," a doll, a teddy bear, or some other favorite toy that can accompany the child into the operating room. My new son chooses to carry his well-worn photo album. When I am ushered into the recovery room, I find Yuanjun showing all the nurses pictures of his new home.

With Yuangun's usual good grace and plenty of handholding, he comes through the surgery amazingly well. Like young royalty, he lays enthroned in his hospital bed when his brothers and sisters come to see him.

When it is time to come home, our prince rides in a wheelchair, casts up to his hips. As we reach our wooded lane, Yuanjun sits up straighter and peers out the car window. He seems to hold his breath, releasing it only when the house appears in view. "*Wo she xiangjia,*" he whispers. "I am homesick." "*Wo-de piao-liang-de jiali.*" "My beautiful house."

Yuanjun can now run and shout as lustily as his brothers and sisters. He fiercely defends his favorite toys, his special books, and his collection of fancy colored pencils. He bangs on the piano, he slams the front door too loudly, and he jumps on his bed. He can crow like a rooster and bellow like a hungry cow. He helps Brendan carry in the milking pails, and he carefully collects the eggs. He still keeps a wide berth of the frisky Yorkshire hogs, but who doesn't? In short, he belongs, and he knows he belongs. He has returned our love; he is family; he is our son. He has never lost his special reverence for our house here at Fern Hill Farm. From time to time, I find him studying the now tattered photo album we sent to China so long ago. He touches the pictures—the pictures of his home.

What is it like for this sturdy and courageous young boy to be suddenly dropped into a family, a country, a home? Let me have Yuanjun tell you. His English, in less than a year, is astounding, but he still speaks of his new home most profoundly in Mandarin. Here is the translation: I come from China to America. I am now a son, a brother. I miss my friends in Shanghai, and sometimes at night I cry. But here—here is my beautiful family; here is my beautiful house.

—Marybeth Lambe

Billy's Prayer

"Are you going to adopt me?" the ten-year-old boy asked. "I've been praying for a real mom and dad. Are you them?"

I didn't know how to answer the skinny little guy with long spindly legs, gangling arms, and a smile brighter than the fluorescent light over our heads. The lady at the child welfare office who had referred us to the Kentucky Children's Home had told us these kids couldn't be adopted because the state had not yet dissolved parental rights. That was okay, because adoption to us meant a baby sometime in the future, not an older child. For now, all we wanted was to sponsor a child for Christmas.

Struggling for the correct answer, I said, "Oh, I wouldn't want you to make such a big decision tonight. You might not like us. But how about coming to our house to visit? Would you like to spend Christmas with us?"

"Yeah," he beamed.

The children's home needed sponsors for the Christmas holidays, and Billy was spending this Christmas with us. We took Billy to the mall for a couple of hours, looking for an insight as to what might please him. "Oh, I want this." He immediately picked up a toy science lab. But soon some action figures seemed more important. Then he settled on a train set.

Later, my husband and I returned for the real shopping. Thinking perhaps we might invite him again for another holiday, we went a bit above the twenty-dollar maximum the orphanage suggested for his gift. We'd keep the excess toys at our house just in case.

On Christmas morning, Billy's eyes glowed and danced in unity with the tree lights. In the course of a few days, the anonymous "ten-year-old child" became an endearing little boy to us. Over the next several months, we continued bringing Billy home with us for holidays, school breaks, and any other excuse we could find. After all, someone should play with all those toys lying around our house.

Each visit ended the same. When it was time to return, Billy would put on his pout face and say,

"Man, is it time to go back there already?" or "Will you come and get me again real soon?"

Even though he was ten years old, he loved sitting on my lap, and every time he caught me sitting down, he would plop himself there. Several visits after his first stay, I took Billy by the hand and pulled him onto my knee. "Hey, I have a surprise for you. How about coming to live with us?" My husband and I had spoken to a social worker about keeping him under the foster-parent program.

"You mean you're gonna adopt me?" He flung his arms around my neck.

"No, Billy, I'm sorry," I answered. "We can't adopt you, but you can live in our house with us."

"Okay!" He jumped and clapped his hands, those brilliant, blue eyes shining like tinsel. "But I'll still pray you'll adopt me so I can have a real family all of my own."

The red tape wasn't too complicated, because we'd been his sponsors for the past ten months. Before the next Christmas, we were officially Billy's foster parents.

Billy had been in two foster homes before he was placed with us, both ending in disaster. This had left him skeptical of foster care, and he found it difficult to accept that we really did love him. One day he came home from school very upset and frightened because he had torn a hole in his new jeans. He was ready for his punishment.

"Don't fret, son, I'll fix them." It was 1971, and patches only made a pair of jeans more valuable. I pulled some scraps of material from my sewing basket and appliquéd a basketball over the hole on the torn leg and stitched a basketball goal on the other.

"Look what my mom did!" He showed them to everybody he encountered. It wasn't long before mysterious little rips and tears "just happened" to all his jeans. I pretended to be shocked, but I smiled as I sewed new patches.

For Easter, I made Billy a navy blue blazer and a pair of matching pants. A red tie completed the outfit. I couldn't get them off him. After he begged and pleaded, I gave in and let him wear the suit to school. The teacher told me he paraded in front of the class, and when the kids teased him about being dressed up, he puffed out his chest and replied, "My mama made this just for me, and I'm gonna wear it every day."

In November, Billy told us he wanted a mini-bike for his birthday. The social service workers gave a definite no. My husband bought him one anyway, and then he called the caseworker and said, "This is the way it's going to be." What else could they do? They didn't want to take Billy back to the home.

The day before his birthday, when I tucked him in and kissed him goodnight, I couldn't help but tell him we had a big surprise for him the next day.

"Just close your eyes and think of what you want the most in the whole world," I said, "and you just might get it."

Billy leaped out of bed and hugged me so tightly that I had to loosen his grip. "You're gonna adopt me! You're gonna adopt me! That's what I want most in the whole world for my birthday! God's done answered my prayers."

When an eleven-year-old wants a family more than anything in the world, how do you justify to him that you can't adopt him? I explained that certain papers had to be signed, and we didn't have those papers. "We have a gift for you that you'll like better anyway." I tried to sound cheerful.

Billy, who had become accustomed to covering up disappointments, just shrugged his shoulders and fell asleep.

Then I cried.

The next day, he was so excited over that mini-bike. He rode it up and down the creek banks and around the house like a miniature Evel Knievel. He didn't mention adoption.

After the birthday celebration was over, I made a call to Mrs. Smith, the social worker in charge of

Billy's placement. "You need to help me explain to this little boy why I can't adopt him. He told me that was all he wanted for his birthday, and I was forced to tell him no. That's just not fair," I told her.

"But, Mrs. Kinsey, I thought you knew," she replied. "Billy's parents signed away all legal rights at the time the courts took him away. It's true that this home is not for adoptable children. However, he was in the home because we had no other placement for him. Because he's both epileptic and his emotional problems sometimes get out of control, we couldn't find a placement for him. That's how he ended up here."

We initiated adoption procedure immediately. By Christmas 1973, Billy had a family of his own, and we had a son. Billy's prayer was answered.

—*Jean Kinsey*

The Zit

After months of waiting, it's finally the day. And I have this zit. This is not supposed to happen in your thirties, but the stress of the past few months has catapulted me back to adolescence, and I am facing the bane of my youth, the zit.

We are on the thruway heading to the airport. The threatening November sky reflects the mood in the car. My cousin Barbara and her husband Jack are driving, knowing we would be incapable of getting there on our own. They've always been there for us, but they are nervous, making small talk, envisioning all sorts of disasters, knowing that my husband or I could shatter with just one setback. Tony and I sit in the back seat, silent, barely breathing, afraid to hope.

Scott has been gone sixteen months now, and every day has been a November day, sad, overcast, and bleak. The shock of our beautiful twelve-year-old's death in a bicycle accident has taken its toll on our disabled son, Kevin, and on us. Kevin lost his best friend, his loving, patient, and accepting big brother, the only one who included him in ballgames and fun with his friends. Scott's buddies don't come around anymore. The house is quiet, and his parents seldom laugh. Light and fun left the day Scott did. They say there is no worse pain than losing your child, and I cannot imagine a worse sorrow. Every day has been a struggle, our grief bottomless and endless. Most days we don't care if we live or die.

Tony is more the survivor than I am. He knows that our lives are not enough, not for us and not for Kevin. He knows we need more. He wants more children. He still has that rudiment of hope. He makes us swim up out of the hole of despair and take a chance. I resist. I want to protect myself from further hurt. I'm afraid to confront the possibility of new pain, but he pulls me up and out of the pit of hopelessness. He holds me tight as we take the leap of faith.

The medical issues that so hurt Kevin were still with us, so pregnancy was not an option. We investigated several local adoption agencies and searched the "Blue Books," huge volumes of pictures of children waiting for families. We were not eligible for a young child because of our ages, and a black or

Hispanic child would not be placed with a white family. Agencies expressed concern over the issue of Kevin's care and our own vulnerability. We were deeply discouraged.

We went to an International Adoptive Families group meeting and open house and fell in love with the children playing in the room. All hues, all special and beautiful. We knew there was a child in the world who needed us as much as we needed her.

We embarked on the route to foreign adoption. We applied to Parsons Child and Family Center in Albany, New York. We painstakingly filled out the applications, contacted priests and doctors for our references, were given physicals, had our fingerprints taken. Still grieving, we spent months with our hearts in our throats and on our sleeves, fearful of missteps, lost visas, and scrutinizing home studies. We met every setback with anxiety and fear, but we were finally rewarded with a grainy black and white 3x5 picture of a six-week-old baby girl with somber black eyes and a mop of straight black hair. In the photo, she is sitting on her foster mother's lap, fingers open, reaching. We open the doors to our hearts and take her in.

In the weeks that follow, that picture was always in our hearts. Copies decorated the refrigerators of our family and friends. We would get updates from Parsons and Korea about her health, her immunizations, even the condition of her bowel movements, but our baby was only getting older, thousands of miles away from us, from our care. But today is the day; she is on her way home. It is Kevin's tenth birthday, and we've promised him a special present.

When we arrive at JFK, we learn the plane from Korea will be delayed for several hours. Jack drives us to an Italian restaurant, and Tony and I push the food around on our plates. When your stomach is filled with anxiety and fear, there is little room for food. Barbara and I go to the ladies' room, and there, looking back at me, is the zit, bigger and brighter than ever. It almost has a pulse. Barbara is trying for diplomacy. She suggests that I pack it in hot water to pop it, make it less noticeable. I try, but I can't. I'm afraid. For the first time in sixteen months, I want to live! I don't want to die. Please God, not now.

Mary Kate is carried down the jet way and placed in my arms. Her almond eyes look at my flawed face, my vulnerability, and me. I hope she sees unconditional love and acceptance for who she is and who she'll become. I hope she sees a survivor, someone who will teach her that life is not always fair, that beauty is more than skin deep, that she'll be okay. Mary Kate has been given the gift of an imperfect mother.

—Helen Legocki

Particularly Close to His Granny

"Mom" and "Dad" were not familiar words. My mother left when I was a year old, and my father fumbled the job of raising me. He was a prisoner of his mistress—the mix of azure skies and cotton clouds that brew the love nectar called "flying." And like a harlot must do, flying stole him away. He took his aviation skills to war and made his mark crossing "The Hump," flying countless 18,000-foot missions over the Himalayas to protect the Burma Road. He flew alongside Chennault's Flying Tigers as they helped chase the war out of China. This rag-tag assemblage of men later became a fetus of Pan American Airways.

My grandmother, "Granny Liz," became both Mom and Dad—and caretaker of my youth. I rarely saw my father. A pilot's log book and sporadic telegrams bearing his cable address, "Tailwind," were the only words he left me. I kept the telegrams in a shoebox until the thin paper strips became brown and fragile. Eventually, they broke into meaningless chips of the alphabet due to my unfolding and reading them so often.

My father's lifestyle soared as high as his airplane. At the end of every day, he sought out the plenty of his amber companion—that thief of reason cloaked in a brown paper bag. At age forty-one, his battered liver called his name aloud.

The funeral services included a legion of who's-who in the aviation world. His death brought notoriety and headlines to our little East Texas town, and suddenly I was a celebrity by association. For one whole day, I stood rigid at his coffin—a fourteen-year-old sentry guarding the gates to the Pharaoh's tomb. I felt more important in his passing than in his life. The people who paraded by patted my shoulder and muttered words of comfort. I heard somebody whisper "little orphan," and another person said, "I imagine the boy was particularly close to his father."

Amidst the stares and well-meaning voices, one comment stood out. It came from Captain James Maupin, a pilot and soldier of fortune who flew alongside my father much of his career. During a quiet moment, Maupin knelt beside me and said, "Now you have to be the man in Granny's house."

Indeed, I was the man of the house. There was no one left but my grandmother and me. Suddenly I saw her in a new light. She was old and frail, and she had depended on my father so much more than I knew. She had no income, having been deserted by the Social Security system because her husband did not contribute to it before he died. With my father gone, we were cast adrift financially.

Her faith rose above it all. "The Lord will bring forth his tidings," she said.

Somehow, we managed with the proceeds from my father's meager estate and money I earned after-school and summer jobs.

My grandmother did not drive, so when I became fifteen, we traded a good freezer for an old car. I was granted a hardship license and taught myself how to drive. I burned the clutch out in three weeks.

"You've been riding the clutch," the mechanic said. The thirty dollars it took to fix the clutch cured me. I learned to dwell the clutch against the accelerator pressure in perfect synchronization. It saved the clutch but frequently left streaks of rubber from the jackrabbit starts.

The tire man was quick to diagnose: "You've been digging out." He replaced the rear tires with twenty-dollar recaps. I had more to learn.

At home, every meal was strategically planned around the newspaper market specials. If bologna was on sale, we ate broiled bologna steaks or bologna sandwiches. If there was no meat on sale, we feasted on purple-hull peas and Granny Liz's masterful hot-water cornbread. We never wanted.

Saturday was market day, and my grandmother prowled the newspaper specials. Shopping for groceries took most of the day. We bought the specials at A&P and then drove across town to Safeway for the sale items there. Next was Piggly Wiggly for its advertised bananas at five cents per pound. The day ended at Lucky Market, because "They have the freshest ground coffee," Granny Liz said.

As I grew older, I became impatient with the hopscotch shopping and explained to my grandmother that the cost of the gas offset the savings. My treatise was ignored. Once I hid part of the newspaper sale inserts, hoping to eliminate two of the four markets. My grandmother called the *News Chronicle* and complained that we had been shorted the sale ads. They promptly sent out another paper, customer service being what it was in those days.

Those were my "formative years," and grandmothers are trained to recognize which years those are. As a result, I suffered an extraordinary amount of "pew time." We were members of the Presbyterian church, and that commanded three services a week. Granny also shepherded a neighborhood mission, and that meant two additional services.

Five pew-sittings a week were far more than a young man's will or posterior could endure. In time, I began dropping her off and skipping the services, then coming back to pick her up. When she raised the same mathematics about wasted gasoline, I revived my rant about multiple-market shopping. I remember the disappointment in her eyes and how she clenched her teeth to suffer my rebellion. I tried not to reveal it, but skipping church hurt my conscience deeply. I remember how she looked at me and asked, "Can't you stay for one hour of service?" I had to hang my head as I answered, "No."

At seventeen, all my easy rites of passage had been mastered. Two remained. The first was beer. I began my trek down what I call the "Yellow Suds Road" quite innocently. East Texas' famed Caddo Lake was nearby, and I spent free days fishing from a favorite dock. One Saturday I discovered a string tied to the planks. The string led to a potato sack containing a six-pack of beer. Someone had put it there to "weather-cool." Falling back on my religious upbringing, I decided it was a gift from God.

That beer sample was a smorgasbord of joy that nourished all my senses, and I immediately became a regular diner. On cool nights I kept a supply between the window and the screen in my bedroom—a make-do fridge. I cut a small slit in the screen so I could push my empties into the hydrangeas below and then retrieve them at the light of day. This continued until our nosy neighbor, Miss Crain, reported the cache to my grandmother. Miss Crain could see my window from hers and had performed the necessary reconnaissance to determine that the objects in the window were contraband. The tears that welled in my grandmother's eyes once again stirred my slumbering conscience. I gave up beer.

As for my second and last remaining rite of passage, or cosmetic flaw, just call it "displaced angst." A psychiatrist might say that my court-and-conquer mode of romance was a delayed response to mother neglect. If so, I was its poster boy. Although I truly fell in love every time I dated someone, once the hunt and capture ended, I bolted like a thief in the night. I developed a reputation for one-night stands, earning the nickname "Old Ninety-Nine"—a title borrowed from the daily express train to Little Rock.

It all changed when I met Miss Kay. She was so pure, she made me respectable again. I brushed up on my manners and even returned to church. On my eighteenth birthday, Kay gave me a Saint Christopher's medal on a chain. This gift of gold made her parents sense things were getting too serious, and Kay was told she couldn't see me again.

It devastated us. Two Saturdays later, we packed small bags and jumped across state lines into a wild-west jurisdiction that blessed marriages for eighteen-year-olds. For twenty-five dollars, the panting underaged could get a blood test and marriage license and have the ceremony performed in iambic pentameter. I don't remember the words; at some point the judge just poked me in the ribs and told me to say, "I do." We were given a hug and showered with a handful of rice—probably Minute Rice in keeping with the pace of the ceremony.

There were no wedding gifts; society forbids wedding-gift registries for runaways. We started life with a sparsely furnished rental house and some pawnshop cookware. After a few months of peace-making with her parents, Kay and I settled into an average life with a now-extended family.

Soon Granny Liz suffered declining health and strokes. It became necessary for her safety for us to close her home. She declined our full-court press to move her into a spare bedroom of our home.

"Laws of natural order prohibit two cooks in the same kitchen," she said. She was firm in that notion.

We placed her in a boarding house with four other women and a saintly caregiver named Josie O'Leary. My grandmother remained there for four years, enjoying Josie's special attention and a level of personal care normally reserved only for close relatives.

My grandmother died within days of my twenty-eighth birthday. The call from Josie came in the middle of the night, and to this day all late-night phone calls push me into cold sweats. That night, it wasn't a wrong number. The voice was halting, but the message was clear. "Your Granny Liz has passed to her lord," Josie said.

A picture of my grandmother sits on my desk. It is a black-and-white photo taken by a newspaper writer on the occasion of her ninetieth birthday. The writer published a story about her in the *News Chronicle*, recalling her life and what she had witnessed over nine decades. "From Mules to Moon, She Saw It All," the headline read.

In the article, Granny Liz spoke about the saloons that once dotted Main Street, how those streets were just hard-packed dirt and sawdust, and how progress was measured by the spraying of used oil on the streets as their initial paving. She told about the coming of industry—the sprawling railroad shops that provided work to a thousand people and replaced cotton as the principal product of the area. Her story ended with what she called her "final bookend"—the television coverage of the Apollo moon landing on July 20, 1969.

"No other generation, past or future, can mark this amount of progress in just 100 years," she said.

At the time of that newspaper article, I paid less-than-deserved attention to it. Like so many other things I can recall about my life with my grandmother, it was one of far too many moments that I took for granted and now regret not having savored. The greatest malady of youth is thinking there are limitless tomorrows.

Now, I would trade soul and wealth for some brief moments with Granny Liz. I realize that many joys were impatiently squandered. If I could seat her in my car today, I would gladly drive to every market in town to chase bologna and bargain bananas. And as I reflect on it, five times a week in the pew seems just about right.

—Lad Moore

A version of this story was first published under the title "Coffee from My Saucer" in the author's memoir, Odie Dodie, BeWrite Books, 2002, UK.

My *Own* Mother!

The jet boat skimmed the surface of Lake Shasta in Northern California. It was blazing hot. The only things stopping us from melting into the dark-brown, vinyl seats were the speed-induced wind and our wet swimming suits.

Our seventeen-year-old son, Dan, taking his turn in the water, casually leaned back on the skis, allowing himself to be gently pulled along the surface of the water. His confidence was such a happy contrast to the withdrawn five-year-old we'd adopted twelve years earlier.

My husband piloted the boat, and it was my job to watch the skier. If he disappeared in a wave of water and foam, I was to hoist the orange flag and call out, "Skier down!" so we could circle back before we lost track of the little speck of a head in the lake.

Dan clearly had settled into a smooth ride, comfortable in the level, frothy area between the two waves of the wake as they moved apart behind us. He waved to a passing skier, then looked ahead to a little island we were about to pass. I loved just looking at him—slim, blonde, and strong—but my mind wandered.

In contrast, when his brother Mike was out there, I had to watch intently every second. He'd be over the wake and head over heels in an instant, usually bonking his head with one of the skis as he tried some foolhardy trick or another.

Dan and Mike are biological brothers whom we adopted when they were three and five years old, but they couldn't be more different from each other in personality. Dan, the older, had an untreated, congenital heart condition and was so skinny and so shy when we got him. He often hid under the bed and never said a word about what he wanted or what he didn't like. Mike was intense, active, opinionated, and hungry all the time.

Mike had a birthday a month after the adoption, so we gave him a typical kid's birthday party. Cousins and neighbors showed up and played pin the tail on the donkey in the backyard. Presents were everywhere; plenty of cake and ice cream followed off-key singing and candles and, of course, there was the obligatory food fight.

Ten months later, Dan's birthday came around, and we did it all again. He had come out of his shell a little by that time and was positively, if quietly, joyful. That night, when I tucked him in, no longer having to coax him out from under the bed first, he said that he'd hoped all year that he would get a birthday party like Mike's.

I was stunned to realize that he had not just expected it, that he had thought he might not get it. I realized at that moment that he might never feel entirely sure of his place in our family.

Mike pulled me out of my thoughts as he pointed out some deer peeking around three little trees on the shore of that little island. They were calmly looking at our very loud boat as we passed about 100 yards offshore. I picked up my camera to take a picture but first glanced back to see how Dan was doing, fully expecting him to be still leaning back on the skis, looking at the deer as well.

A stab of cold fear knifed through my stomach. Dan wasn't behind the boat. At least five other boats were behind us, speeding back and forth and paying more attention to their own skiers than to what was in the water in front of them. The waves were crazy, with the wakes bouncing off the island.

I shouted to my husband, "Dan's down! I can't see him! Oh, stop! We've got to go back!"

The boat pivoted, ran over its own wake, and threw all of us against the sides and seats as we raced back to locate our downed skier.

We spotted him as he waved his arms to signal his presence to a Jet Ski headed toward him. It had just jumped the wake of a ski boat, and the driver almost lost his balance just a few yards away from Dan. Mike and I waved and hollered, trying to warn the drivers bearing down on Dan from several directions. The Jet Ski turned at the last second, avoiding a dreadful accident with our boy. That action alerted another nearby boat, which then veered away. We had just the moment we needed to get to Dan before anyone else got that close.

When Dan saw it was us coming in at breakneck speed, the panic on his face turned to anger. He was holding both hands in the air, palms facing each other in a jerking motion, as he yelled something I couldn't make out until we got right next to him.

"My own mother! My—*own*—mother!"

Clearly and justifiably, he blamed me, the designated spotter, for putting him into a terrifying position. He'd been alone in that huge lake with speeding water craft whizzing by him because I had been distracted. He was really mad at me—cold, wet, scared, and mad.

With tears in my eyes, I grabbed him and hugged him as soon as he dragged himself up onto the swim platform and into the boat. At first, he tried to push me away. Finally, he gave up and hugged back but just had to repeat one more time, though slightly less angry, "My own mother!" We swayed there for several minutes, him wet and me getting wetter, barely able to stand on the sandy deck of the jet boat as it moved sharply in all directions at once with the wakes of passing boats.

Dan was so angry with me that he could hardly speak to me. But this young man who had once been so unsteady in his self-esteem, so unsure of his place on the planet and within our family, now thinks of me as none other than his own mother.

—*Sallie Wagner Brown*

Meant to Be

The first phone call came during a hectic time in my life. Scrambling to finish a master's degree, decorate a baby's room, and submit an article by deadline, I answered the phone in a fog.

"Mrs. Miller?"

"Yes . . ."

"This is Carol from the agency."

I don't remember much about the call after that. In fact, I have managed to block out most of what happened in the month after that call. A match . . . a boy . . . not connecting with birth parents . . . match falling through.

If the adoption process is like a pregnancy, a match that doesn't survive is like a miscarriage. We wept, we grieved, we grew doubtful, but through the miracle of time, we were able to find hope again. After all, I knew we were really meant to have a little girl.

Like all expectant parents, we shopped. I researched baby products online, wondering which car seat would provide the most safety. Which of the twenty different bottle brands would cause the least amount of gas? Was it the colorful gym mat or the black-and-white choice that would ensure our baby's future academic success?

When the choices became too much, I turned off the computer and set out to rummage sales. It was at one of these sales that I found an antique print of a sleeping baby. I brought it home to hang above the crib. Now, all we needed was the sleeping baby in the crib.

Weeks later, the second call came.

"Hello?"

"Mrs. Miller?" Not a match, but a request. Could the agency send our profile to a young couple on the West Coast?

This baby was due a month after my graduation. They did not know the gender yet, but I knew it was a girl. This baby was The One.

The next couple weeks were probably the longest of our lives. Thank goodness, I had final papers to write and more deadlines to meet. I called my husband at work almost daily just to talk. "Can you believe it? We are going to be parents!" "What should we do about a name?" "Who should we call first to announce our wonderful news?"

My heart jumped when the phone rang late one night. Our agency was on West Coast time. We ran to different phones to pick up a receiver.

"Hi, Donna. Hi, Frank. Sharon again. I have great news. Are you ready? The couple chose you!"

I don't know how many heartbeats that muscle is allowed to safely make in your body during a minute's time, but I think mine came close to setting some kind of record.

We were nervous about the call to Gina and Tom, the birth parents. It would be a three-party call to include the agency, and Sharon would ask most of the questions. This would be the most important blind date of our lives.

It seems cliché to boast when you know right away that something is right, but that's just what happened the night of that phone call. Gina and Tom were our soulmates, a brother and sister in another lifetime.

Sharon continued to talk with us after Gina and Tom hung up, coaching us about the process afterward. She agreed that the conversation went really well and was certain it would result in a match.

Then Sharon gave us more information. Prior to being offered our profile, the birth parents had chosen another couple for their child, but it turned out that couple had wanted a girl. This baby was a boy.

She also told us that she probably wasn't supposed to have called us about this baby. Because our previous match had not worked out, a note had been placed in our file to give us some time before setting up another match. Sharon was new to the agency and had not seen that note.

Before hanging up, Sharon let us know that Gina's birthday was coming up.

"Oh, really?" I said. "What is the date?"

"June 26." I nearly dropped the phone. June 26 is my birthday.

Our little guy recognized us the moment we saw him. Born only hours before, his eyes grew wide and his gaze rarely left ours. The month after that was a blur of hotel rooms, plane trips, baby bottles, burping, diapers, and little sleep. But one quiet night is forever engraved on my heart. While watching over our beautiful baby boy asleep in his crib, I studied that antique print again. The sleeping baby, as angelic and peaceful as our own at that moment, was snuggled in a blanket. I smiled while I stared at the color of that blanket. It was blue.

—Donna Morin Miller

The Talk: Part One in a Series

"Was I in your tummy, too, Mommy?"

I can't say that this question from Peyton arrived sooner or later than I expected. I just knew it would come some time after she realized that babies, and not beach balls, grew inside pregnant women's bodies, which was roughly a year ago. But I guess she wasn't old enough then to make a connection between those unborn babies and the baby she had once been or between those women and me.

She did make the connection between her baby-self and her older sister Taylor's baby-self, though, when Taylor asked me recently to tell the story—again—about how her dad used to tap on my belly when I was pregnant with her and she would tap back.

That's when Peyton asked, "Was I in your tummy, too, Mommy?"

It's very important these days for Peyton to be as much like Taylor as possible. At restaurants, she orders whatever Taylor orders. If Taylor gets dressed up for some occasion, Peyton must be in her Sunday best too; otherwise, she wails and writhes as if we've suggested sending her outside nude in the snow. If Taylor doesn't like a particular flavor of gum, Peyton removes the piece she had been happily chewing from her mouth and declares it "yucky." Thank God for Target and Payless, where I can find reasonably priced, age-appropriate identical clothes and shoes in both their sizes. Thank God for Taylor, age eight, who doesn't yet mind dressing like her baby sister.

So it followed that when Taylor talked about being in my stomach, Peyton asked if she'd been there too.

Without missing a beat, I replied, "No, honey. You weren't in my tummy. You were in a different mommy's tummy, and after you were born, we brought you home to live with us"—just as I'd rehearsed in my head for the past three years or so. A straightforward, short answer, just as the adoption books recommended for a child her age.

While I silently patted myself on the back for coming across so relaxed and cool, my heart pounded in my chest and my mouth went dry. I hadn't rehearsed what to say next.

Taylor to the rescue. "Yeah, we flew on a plane to Chicago and picked you up, and you were so cute, and you cried like this: 'Ah-geeeee, Ah-geeeee, Ah-geeeee!'"

Peyton giggled and went back to eating her cheese and crackers.

Later that evening, I searched the house for *How I Was Adopted*, a picture book by Joanna Cole (of *The Magic School Bus* fame). I couldn't find it anywhere. I had hidden this book to make sure Taylor or a well-meaning babysitter didn't read it to Peyton. I'd read it to her once when she was about eighteen months old, along with *The Snowy Day* and *The Runaway Bunny*, as just another bedtime book. My ex, Mike, and I felt that we should be the ones to reintroduce this book to her once she had a rudimentary understanding of adoption.

Mike and I had talked about being matter-of-fact about Peyton's adoption. And we decided that we wanted her to say, as we've heard some adult adoptees say, "It seems like I've always known that I was adopted." We knew that being adopted might mean everything and nothing to Peyton and that her feelings about it were likely to change as she entered various stages of her life—school-age, adolescence, adulthood, motherhood. We wanted to offer her a blank slate on which to write that story for herself.

We wouldn't tell her that she was lucky or better off being adopted. We'd state the facts, answer her questions as best and as honestly as we can, and affirm that we love her. The conclusions were hers to draw.

But that is all yet to come. Now, I had to find that missing book. *How I Was Adopted* was supposed to be the big follow-up to The Question, and I had somehow managed to hide it from myself.

I told Mike about Peyton's question, and we agreed that it was time to get more books. Throughout our fifteen years together, books were our answer to everything. Marital problems? Read how-to-stay-together books. Pregnancy and childbirth? Keep eight baby books on the nightstand at all times. Parenting? Own the complete Dr. Sears library. Divorcing? Buy two copies of *How to Get Divorced Without Ruining Your Life*. So, while I ordered a replacement copy of *How I Was Adopted*, Mike picked up several other titles.

He ordered books for right now, like Jamie Lee Curtis's *Tell Me Again About the Night I Was Born*, with its comforting repetition, and he ordered books for when Peyton is older, like *Adoption Is for Always*, whose cover features a somber-faced little girl named Celia. Like us, Celia's parents had told her that she was adopted from the time she was "a tiny girl" and that she'd "grown inside a lady called her *birth mother.*" But Celia hadn't understood. When her parents told her they adopted her, it had no more significance than when they said, "We took you to the park when you were a baby."

When Celia is old enough to grasp what adopted means, at first she is sad and angry. When we find ourselves at that point with Peyton, it will be Taylor to the rescue again. Shortly after Mike and I told her we were divorcing, Taylor coined the term *smad.* "I feel sad and mad," she'd said. When (if?) Peyton becomes smad, we'll ride that wave with her, being as understanding as we can, creating a safe place for her to vent, within boundaries, as Celia's parents do.

Besides that, and continuing to be forthright, I really don't know how to rehearse for the second and subsequent parts of The Talk. I know the questions will get harder. Why, Peyton will ask, did her birth mother place her for adoption? Where is her birth mother now, and can she see her? Why, she might ask even later, did her father and I adopt a child, only to separate less than two years later? Biological facts are simple; emotions and motivations and "grown-up problems" not so much. Sometimes, I recite the answers in my head, but even then, it's not easy. I want Peyton to know that she was loved by her birth mother and that she is loved by us now and always. I want her to understand and feel secure in this love. I want so badly for her not to hurt, not to feel unwanted. I want things that rest only partly in my hands.

I guess I'll have heart palpitations along that bridge when I come to it. For now, we read about Sam (short for Samantha) and how she was adopted. At the end of the book, Sam asks, "Do you know the story of how you were adopted?" Every time, Peyton answers, "Yes!" And she really does. She knows her birth mother's name, that we brought her home on an airplane, that all our friends and family threw a big party at our house to welcome her, and that we love her very much.

"Was I in your tummy, too, Mommy?"

"No, sweetie, you weren't. But you've been right here in my heart since the day I first held you. And that's where you'll always be."

And I can hear Peyton saying, "Just like Taylor?"

"Yes, just like Taylor."

—Deesha Philyaw

To Be Chosen

My parents, Irv and Pat, live on the Gulf Coast of Florida, on a spring-fed river surrounded by tall pines and Spanish moss, alligators and manatees, and flocks of snowbirds migrating south from their Yankee homelands. They live in a small town called Weeki Wachee. Perhaps you've heard of it: "Weeki Wachee, Home of the Live Mermaids." The roadside attraction of the same name is legendary; it's been around since I was a kid. They actually have real-live mermaids, underwater, with oxygen hoses you're not supposed to see, and when I was a kid I never did.

But Irv and Pat are not my first parents. Adoption runs in my family. Irv adopted me at birth; I adopted Pat as an adult.

I was adopted through a doctor's office back in 1958 by Irv and his first wife, Joan. An unwed teenager had been sent to Florida to have her baby. Whatever she had, Irv and Joan would get. They got me! Two years later, they got Mike, and six years after that, when I was eight, they got divorced.

Irv and Joan both remarried, but I always considered them to be my parents and the people they married to be my stepparents, whom I referred to by their first names. As for the unwed teenager sent away to have her baby, I think I may have inherited some of her tenacity, but I never considered her to be my parent.

Irv and Joan had a book called *The Chosen One*, a Dick-and-Jane-type primer intended to explain the concept of adoption to young children. Someone had gone through the entire book and meticulously drawn a line through Mr. and Mrs. Brown's last name and written our family's name in its place. The names of the two adopted children had been replaced with those of my brother Mike and me.

I didn't grow up thinking I was unwanted or unloved. I grew up knowing I was chosen.

But Joan had a habit of embarrassing me, of emasculating me in front of friends and family, at Little League games and school functions, and, of course, directly to my face.

When I was a toddler—a fat, happy toddler— Joan hung a sign around my neck that said "Do Not

Feed Me" and sent me out to play. When I was six, I had a best friend named Kyle. Joan said it was a "queer" name and that I was not to be his friend anymore. I didn't even know what the word meant, but she was adamant and her point was clear. (Ironically, when I was in my twenties and came out as a gay man, Joan didn't seem to have any problem with it.)

Then there was the time Joan and her new husband took the family to see the film *Paint Your Wagon*. I was twelve and thought it was going to be a western, with cowboys and Indians, maybe a scalping or two. Imagine my surprise when it turned out to be a musical—featuring drunken miners and saloons and whores, no less. I don't think I'd even remember it if it weren't for the part where the scruffy old miners took the young kid into his first cathouse. That's when Joan leaned over to me and whispered, "That'll be just like you. The first girl you ever have sex with, and you'll get her pregnant!" I don't remember anything after that. I have no idea if the young kid found the whore of his dreams or if he got her pregnant or if drunken miners broke into song about it. I just remember what Joan said.

Three years later, I entered my first speech contest, a countywide competition sponsored by the

Rotary Club. The title of my speech was "I'm Just One." I wrote about being an individual, and I won. After the contest, as the runners up and I posed with our plaques and our savings bonds, I overheard Joan holding court with a small group of parents standing beside the stage. I listened as Joan told complete strangers how her first thought had been "Just one what?" She laughed at the possibilities; I smiled for the cameras.

Fast-forward twenty years: I was living in Los Angeles and had flown Joan out from North Carolina to visit me for her birthday. We were having brunch at a nice restaurant, just the two of us, sitting outside at a sidewalk table, when I decided to ask her about some of the things she had done and said when I was growing up. When I finished my *Paint Your Wagon* story, Joan looked at me and said, "What a terrible thing to say. Why would I say such a terrible thing?"

"Good question," I replied. "Why would you?"

I wanted to feel sorry for her, maybe even forgive her, but there was no acknowledgment. No hint of remorse. No blanket apology to assuage my hurt. No nothing.

"So what's good here?" she asked, turning her attention back to the menu and away from what was in front of her.

It didn't matter. The damage had been done.

It's hard to explain why we aren't close to someone. It's never just one thing; it's a lifetime of little things. But in the end, it's the love we get from one that we don't get from another that seems to make the difference. Maybe it was the blood-bond that Joan and I didn't share that allowed me to divorce her and adopt Pat—whom Dad married in 1975—in her place. I'm not sure. I'm also not sure it really matters. What does matter was the soul-searching I did and the decision I made, for which I have no regrets.

It was *The Chosen One* all over again, except this time it was written from the little boy's point of view. I was thirty-eight years old, and I had chosen Pat.

Unlike my first adoption, this one couldn't be run through a doctor's office. I had to hire an attorney, file papers with the court in Florida, where I was born, and have the matter set for hearing. I also had to send a notice of the hearing to Joan and give her the chance to object. It turns out Joan not only had the right to object, she had the right to turn an otherwise simple proceeding into something messy and expensive.

I didn't want Joan finding out about this from the afternoon mail. She needed to hear it from me. I needed to call her. I don't remember how many false starts or Xanax it ultimately took, but I made the call, and it was just as horrible as I had imagined it would be. The news came as a shock; she couldn't understand what she had done to make me go to such an extreme. I remember telling her, with complete sincerity, that it wasn't something I was doing to her; it was something I was doing for myself.

Knowing Joan, I'm sure she didn't hear a word I said, but in the end she did not object. She did, however, ask if we could remain "friends" and stay in touch a couple of times a year. We haven't spoken since.

That was 1996. I began my adoption proceeding in July of that year, and two months later, Pat was diagnosed with stage-three colon cancer. While she was in the hospital, Pat told her oldest daughter, Michelle, that she hoped I would continue with the adoption, because she "would be honored" to be my mother.

She would be honored to be my mother? When I heard that I cried.

By Christmas, my adoption was done. The court order was signed, my new birth certificate was being issued, and Pat—I mean, Mom—was preparing for fifty-two weeks of aggressive chemotherapy. A year later, when chemo was complete and the worst appeared to be over, Dad was diagnosed with prostate cancer. They decided on an experimental treatment, combining three different plans of medical attack, and suddenly their roles as caretaker and patient were reversed. But in typical Irv-and-Pat fashion, they turned their lemons into lemonade, and once again the rest of us were left to marvel at the two of them.

Dad always says there is nothing more valuable in life than experience (and, of course, family), and he and Mom continue to create new experiences every day. They are partners, lovers, best friends, and as anyone who knows them will tell you, inspirational . . . whether they're cleaning the river behind their home or swimming in it with their grandchildren, driving through Spain or sailing themselves through the Caribbean, where they once lived. Nothing stops them.

They so enjoyed Costa Rica on their first visit that they moved there for four months to immerse themselves in the culture. On their last night, masked men with machetes broke into their villa and attacked them. They were beaten, bound, blindfolded, and thrown into a mosquito-infested swamp. Every time they tried to get up, the sharp tip of a machete pushed them back down into the muck. Throughout their ordeal, two of their attackers kept shouting, *"Mátelos! Mátelos!"* "Kill them! Kill them!" But a third attacker—a voice they recognized from the village, a man whose daughter they had helped plan a birthday party for—mercifully refused to let that happen.

They came home traumatized but alive, and within a year they were planning their next trip, to Thailand and Burma and then to Australia and New Zealand. Dad said it sounded like an incredible experience and too good of a deal to pass up. Those are my parents—living every day to the fullest!

A few years ago, I decided to change my last name. It is one of those funny names that everyone gets wrong; even my dad changed the pronunciation of it when I was in college. I thought I might take my mother's maiden name, Mills. Jeff Mills. I liked the sound of it: it was nice, simple, and had a certain daytime soap opera quality I found strangely appealing.

Mom beamed with pride at my announcement. Dad, on the other hand, just nodded slowly, letting the impact of my words sink in.

"Well, I'll tell you," he said calmly. "I would just hate for someone not to know that you were my son."

In a moment of clarity I will remember for the rest of my life—one of those light-bulb moments Oprah always talks about—I realized what my father was telling me: I would hate for anyone not to know they were my parents. I didn't say that, of course. I just nodded slowly, like my father, letting the impact of his words sink in.

"Fine," I said calmly. "I'll keep the damned name."

I watched as my father fought to stifle his growing smile, attempting to remain humble in his shining moment of victory, but it didn't last long, and soon we were all laughing.

Parents love their children; it's a requirement. But when parents are actually proud of you, when they're honored to call you their son, it's a rare and precious gift. And when you're gay, sadly, it's a gift that's often never given. I'm one of the lucky ones—one of the chosen ones—and I'm blessed with wonderful parents. My parents are my role models, they mean the world to me, and their names are Irv and Pat.

—Jeff Buppert

An Answer, Without Question

The look on the doctor's face said it all. Her smile disappeared, and her eyebrows furrowed as she looked at the ultrasound. My gaze turned to the neon images on the screen. A few weeks earlier, I'd seen the beginnings of a human form and the bright bleep, bleep, bleep of a heartbeat. Now, I saw a lifeless blob and felt a sickening churn in my stomach.

"I'm sorry," she said. "I have to go; I'm already late. They're waiting for me downstairs to start a procedure. It will probably take your body a little while to realize . . . Call me if you have any problems."

"It's okay," I tried to reassure myself as much as her. This wasn't my first miscarriage. I'd dealt with these emotions before. But losing a baby is not something I'd gotten used to. I vowed not to cry until I got home.

On our living room sofa, my husband and I sobbed together. I'd thought this pregnancy was the answer to my prayers. After the death of my parents, a previous miscarriage, two surgeries, and a failed attempt at adoption, I deserved an answer. I'd begged God for this baby's life. Now I was facing more questions and answers I didn't want to consider.

Why me? Do you hate me, God? Have I done something to evoke your wrath? I prayed.

It was almost ironic. Prior to these events, I'd been so happy. In sunny Florida, Tony and I were enjoying married life in a neat, four-bedroom house with our daughter, Alexandra. Our financial circumstances allowed me to work part-time as a physical therapist just ten minutes from home. Career, family, home—I had it all.

Only one thing was missing: we wanted another baby.

Once Allie was out of diapers, we decided it was time to try for another child. I'd conceived Alexandra easily, and the only complication had been the need for a Cesarean section rather than a natural birth. So we did not anticipate any reproductive problems, and indeed, all went smoothly . . . at first.

After only two months, I was pregnant.

Then, on an August evening while sewing a loose jumper for my expanding belly, I received a telephone call from my brother in Chicago.

Mike's voice hesitated. "I'm afraid I have some bad news."

I immediately thought of Mom. When I was five, she'd been diagnosed with lupus, and I grew up enduring her frequent trips to hospitals. Somehow, though, she always managed to get better, but I knew someday she would not.

"Mom died, didn't she?" I asked Mike.

"No . . . Dad died."

I let my brother's words sink in. My father hadn't been ill. He worked as a tool and die maker past retirement age, caring for my mother during the day and working the night shift. He was just about to retire at age seventy.

"The neighbors discovered him on the back porch in the rain. He must have had a heart attack while watching a storm come in."

My thoughts drifted back to childhood. Our whole family often sat on the porch of our Chicago home enjoying the brisk wind as a storm approached. We'd marvel at the rapidly moving clouds until it was no longer safe to remain outdoors.

I decided to fly to Chicago alone, not wanting to disrupt Allie's routine. "Besides," I told my husband, "chasing a two-year-old around a funeral home isn't practical."

On the plane, I worried about my mother, who was in the hospital. Dad had called me a week earlier when he couldn't rouse Mom enough to get her out of bed, and I'd encouraged him to take her there.

"How are we going to tell Mom?" I asked my sister, as we drove to her home from the airport.

Alice looked at me sorrowfully. "Oh, honey, we won't have to. She's unresponsive. We can visit her tonight if you'd like. The doctor asked me if I wanted a feeding tube put in, and I gave him the go-ahead. I want her to have food and medicine."

I nodded. My sister is a registered nurse; I trusted her opinion.

"I also told him not to resuscitate her if her heart stops."

That night, I accompanied Alice to the hospital. My mother lay still against stark white sheets. I recognized her face, the familiar curly gray hair, the bump on her nose that resembled my own. I remember how she'd supported my decision to move to Florida. Though sad to let her youngest go, she valued my happiness more than her comfort.

I took my mother's hand, wanting to see whether it looked like the hand I used to hold as a child. I gently squeezed it, then placed my other hand on her chest and rubbed. "Mom?" I called, trying to wake her. "Mom!" I called again, rubbing a little harder.

I looked at my sister, and she shook her head, certain that Mom was not going to respond. I knew Mom loved me and would be excited to see me, that she would wake up if she could. Though I wanted to keep trying, the sad look in my sister's eyes stopped me.

"The nurses don't get any reaction. Dad was the only one who could get her to eat. He used to come and feed her every night."

We made small talk for a while, Mom a silent witness to our conversation.

"You ready to go?" Alice finally asked.

I was not. First, I needed to take one long last look at my mother. She didn't move. Her face showed no expression. Finally, "We can go now," I said.

My siblings made most of the arrangements for Dad's funeral. Maybe because I was pregnant, they decided to leave me out of it. Or maybe because I was the youngest. Either way, I was grateful. Mike acted as my personal chauffeur to all events. On the second night of my father's wake, Mike returned me to my hotel. I'd barely settled in when the phone rang. I answered to hear my sister's strained voice, and I could tell she'd been crying.

"Mom died tonight. The hospital was trying to reach us, but we were at the funeral home."

Our mother had passed away only three days after our father. I thought about Jesus rising in three days, and I envisioned Dad rising and visiting Mom in her coma. "Come on, what are you hanging on for?" he said in my vision, using the impatient tone of voice he always used when trying to motivate her to see his point of view.

I caressed the pregnant bump on my belly, worrying about the baby within. *I hope you're okay in there.* The next day was Dad's funeral. The following day, Mom's wake. A day later, her funeral. Surrounded by friends and family, I felt strangely comforted as they reminisced and took care of me.

Once home in Tampa, I resumed my usual routine. A week later, I began bleeding and suffered my first miscarriage.

"It had to be all that stress," I told the doctor.

As the months passed, I did not resume my monthly cycles and sensed that something was terribly wrong. I saw a specialist, who discovered that my Cesarean section left my womb and abdomen so badly scarred that I needed two corrective surgeries.

After the second surgery, when the serious nature of my condition became apparent, we decided to look into adoption. It was expensive, we discovered, but I inherited just the right sum from my parents' estate. Arrangements were made to adopt a baby boy. After his birth, his birth mother changed her mind.

Throughout these trials, my husband and I cried frequently. Still, I carried on for Alexandra's sake.

And I was determined to make our dreams come true. The very next month, I was pregnant again. *Please, please, please God, let this one live. We have been through so much,* I prayed incessantly.

But when my prayers weren't answered, after looking at the lump of tissue that used to be a life on the ultrasound screen that day in the doctor's office, I began to consider the possibilities. God doesn't listen to me anymore. Worse yet, God hears me but chooses not to act. Then I thought that if I lose my faith, even after suffering so many losses, I lose everything.

Another attempt at adoption failed. A full reproductive work-up led my doctor to the conclusion that all my pregnancies would end in miscarriage. The tone of my prayers became bitter, hostile. *Okay, God, if you don't want me to be a parent again, fine, be that way,* I grumbled. *I can live with one child. I can spoil her rotten, if that's what you want.*

In my heart, though, I knew better. *No matter what, I still believe in you,* I prayed. *And if you don't mind, could you send me a couple of signs you still care about me?*

The adoption attorney's office called again. They had a birth mother for me to consider.

After listening to the profile, I asked the case worker, "What do you think?" I had given up.

She thought it was a good situation.

This is the last one, I told God.

We met the birth mother and the obstetrician's nurse. Together, they were praying for a solution to the birth mother's dilemma.

A month later, I received a phone call at work. The baby was ready to be born. Several hours later, I got another phone call; a baby girl was waiting for us.

Adopting a child is not like achieving parenthood through conventional means. There are not nine months to plan. No baby showers. No names picked out in advance. On the drive to the hospital, we telephoned relatives and entertained suggestions. My sister-in-law suggested Samantha, a favorite name of my husband's late mother. I didn't particularly like the name; Tony did. I thought it only fair he name one child. I chose Alexandra's name.

After arriving at the hospital, we spoke briefly to the birth mother. Then we were ushered into a room where the baby was waiting to be fed.

"It is important that you bond with the baby," the nurse told us.

I lifted the newborn's head covered with fine brown hair. As she eagerly sucked down a bottle of formula, a tear ran down Tony's cheek. That night, her birth mother relinquished parental rights. We returned to the hospital the next day and took Samantha home.

A few days later, I telephoned my sister to tell her about our new addition.

"What's her birthday?" Alice asked, as if she had a pen and calendar in hand, ready to be the doting aunt and send birthday cards for the rest of Samantha's life.

When I told her, she gasped. "That was Mom's birthday."

I was never good about remembering my late mother's birthday. I had not made the connection. Little Samantha was born on the birthday of the woman whose inheritance made her adoption possible. Perhaps there's a divine plan, after all.

A few years later, in preparation for teaching a children's Sunday school class, I was reading the story of Hannah in the Bible. Hannah poured out her heart to God and begged him for a child. She finally conceived and gave birth to a son. She named him Samuel, because in Hebrew it means "asked of God."

Samantha, the feminine form of Samuel, the name I didn't like or choose for my daughter, has its origin in a story about God granting a desperate woman's request. Now, I had all the answers I needed.

—*Ruth E. Jones*

Flossy, Flossy

The phone rings near midnight, and I know it's my daughter calling from Lake Tahoe. Frenzied drums and synthesizers and adolescent screams vibrate in the background.

"G – L – A – M –" I recognize the letters first and then the music. "– O – R – O – U – S . . ."

Katie screams into the phone, "Can you hear it, Mom?"

"Yes, sweetie. I hear it."

We sing the next line of the song together.

"Okay. Gotta go. Just wanted you to hear it. Love you."

"Love you, too, babe."

The connection breaks. I straighten my quilt, fluff my pillows, and settle back into place.

Katie won a radio contest—two airplane tickets, two nights hotel accommodations, and two tickets to see Fergie in concert at Harvey's Outdoor Amphitheatre in Lake Tahoe. She called from the airport, from the hotel room, from her sixteenth-row seats. She's twenty now, and even though she wants to do this on her own, she wants to share it with me, too.

Gratitude washes over me. I could have missed this, all of this.

Somewhere in this world, probably somewhere in the United States, another woman sleeps without interruption. No phone call breaks into her dreams tonight; no rush of love forces her breath into the dark room to mingle with the air beyond the window screens. My daughter's birth mother does not know our girl is on her very first trip without parents, does not know how brave and resourceful that girl has grown to be.

Earlier in the spring, Katie and I had driven around town with the top down on my VW Bug, screeching "Glamorous" at the top of our lungs and hitting replay the moment the last note faded. We'd laughed endlessly at nothing and everything. It's our trademark, that easy laughter. That, and absolute trust in one another.

Katie came into our family when she was five weeks old, a tiny, bald infant with a green bow taped to her oversized head. Oh, that head. For nearly a year our pediatrician fretted about the size of her head, testing and retesting her for scary conditions like brain cancer and hydrocephalus. Even though I'm a chronic worrier, I never fretted, not even while we waited for the results of ultrasounds and then CAT scans and then MRIs.

"Look at her eyes," I'd say. "There's nothing wrong with my baby's brain. She's bright as can be. Watches everything that moves."

I trusted those bright eyes and that gummy smile, and I was right.

When Katie developed asthma and reactive airways at ten months, she trusted me to soothe her croupy cough in a steamy bathroom and later to ease her struggle to breathe with a nebulizer. At eighteen months, she managed to get hold of her asthma medication and drink the whole bottle straight down and then trusted me to keep her safe while the doctors put a tube down her button nose. I sat with my head through the bars of her hospital crib, singing "My Favorite Things" over and over again. Despite everything, she "buzzed" on cue with each "When the bee stings."

Through the years I trusted her to behave at sleepovers, to do her best at school, to use her head with boys. She trusted me to make things okay again after her father and I divorced.

When she was sixteen, we trusted each other to work through the dramatic onset of type 1 diabetes. We learned to count carbs and estimate units of insulin. She peed on sticks, and we compared their color to the charts they gave us at the clinic. That first night, when she cried, "Mom, I'm scared," I trusted her with the truth. "I'm scared, too, honey. But we'll figure it out. Together, we can do anything, even this."

One spring day, two or three years before we first heard "Glamorous," we had lunch together. We sat on the patio of a local restaurant, reveling in the weak spring sun as only true Northerners can. The aroma of hamburgers drifted from the grill, and Katie's stomach growled loudly. We laughed and waved the waiter over to take our order.

"So," I said. "You know we got a letter from your birth mother. Do you want to write her back?"

"No. Not yet. Could you write and tell her about me?" Katie said.

"Of course. But are you sure you don't want to do it?"

"If I do, she'll want to meet me."

"Probably. Is that a bad thing?" I asked.

"No. I'll want that someday, but not yet."

We sat in silence for a minute or two. The breeze picked up, and I unfurled the big cotton napkin onto my lap, grateful for its slight warmth. Katie pulled up the neck of her fuzzy green sweater and drew her arms into its sleeves.

"The thing is," she finally said. "I'm not ready yet. I'm not mature enough. But I will be someday, and when I'm ready, you'll help me."

"You bet I will," was all I could say without crying.

I think of all this as I crawl out of my cover nest and close the window. I'm tired but happy for my daughter. With my daughter. This is what I dreamed of, what carried me through all the tests, procedures, drugs, miscarriage, and seven years on a waiting list.

When we went through the home study, we were asked why we wanted children. Even then, long before Rafiki lifted Simba to the skies in The Lion King, before Elton wrote the song, before I fully understood what it meant, I wanted to be part of the Circle of Life. I wanted to nurture an infant, to see the world through the eyes of a toddler, to learn to read with a young child. God help me, I even wanted to ride the roller coaster of adolescence. I imagined myself in middle age with young adults coming home for holidays. I stepped into the comfy shoes of an old lady baking cookies with grandchildren. I didn't want just babies; I also wanted to share my life with the people those babies would become.

And I am. I hum as I drift back to sleep, "Oh, the flossy, flossy . . ."

—*Jerri Farris*

Ready or Not . . .

I wasn't sure what my children expected when I booked our homeland tour to South Korea. More self-aware than many teens their age, they were adolescents nonetheless—which is to say, given to opacity. My daughter, a priestess of Asian pop—from manga and anime to J-rock—claimed she was going for the fashions. My son, who posed as an Asian no-wannabe after years of inhaling toxic slurs (in our über-educated suburb), said he was interested in being there—as in, being Korean in Korea.

I wondered, however, if either of them knew what they truly hoped to find.

My own goal was simple: to see where they were born. I was not bothered by having (twice) missed the creation, but I felt remiss in not knowing where the creation occurred. The sites listed on the adoption documents, with their variant spellings and ambiguous roles, meant (dare I admit it?) nothing to me. In that sense, you could say I went searching for meaning. In lieu of meeting my children's birth mothers—the Mount Everest of homeland expeditions—I focused on finding birthplaces.

To my surprise, the latter proved elusive; whereas meaning met up with us at every turn, most notably on a street corner in Pusan.

My husband Chris and I first held Lee Jin Ho in Baltimore/Washington International Airport. Lee was one of a half dozen babies delivered at the gate that midnight. Sprouting Munchkinesque tufts of hair at his temples, he looked like a rookie in the Lollipop League. Two years later, at Washington National Airport, we cradled our four-month-old daughter, Park Sun Joo. Julia—who lacked hair altogether but had stunning, take-it-all-in eyes—arrived with a three-year-old boy who spoke only Korean. Because his new parents spoke only English, I wondered how they would cope.

As world travelers, Chris and I looked forward to learning all about our children's heritage. Lee and Julia, however, taught us otherwise: They wanted nothing to do with it. At adoption agency events, in particular, they acted bored or acted up. One day, when we went shopping at a local Korean grocery, I suddenly understood why.

"Am I going to meet my birth mother here?" Julia blurted out, hanging back.

Nonplussed, I assured her, "No, she's not here"—only to feel the fraud. For all I knew, my daughter's mother was the clerk who rang up our noodles and *nori*.

And I wished she were.

In time, the children came to trust that Frosty the Snowman would be built in hell before Chris and I would "send them back," that the four of us formed our own integral family, and that, come what may, we were together for life. No one imagined that life might prove a weak link, that life might abandon us all.

Chris died when Lee was fourteen and Julia was twelve.

Lee grieved pretty much the way I did: spewing emotion, as if he'd taken an emetic to vomit up poison. Day after day, week after week, he tried, in vain, to return to school. I despaired: *Would he ever have the stomach for life again? Would I?* Roiling with anger, he lamented one day, "If my birth father hadn't given me away, I never would have lost Dad."

I couldn't argue with that. If Chris hadn't swept me away in college, I never would have lost him either. Yet, at least we'd found someone worth the anguish. When Chris went missing, I realized how privileged I was to have been loved. That was the irrevocable trust—rather than the one established by his will— that would support us all in perpetuity. From Lee's bitter kernel of truth, however, I saw a new tendril of connection sprouting: to his birth father. Never before had Lee acknowledged his existence.

For Julia, the bereavement was so big and close, she could not make it out. Think: watching a horror film with your nose against the screen. A year passed without her shedding a tear. Then Chris's company invited us to the dedication of a fountain in his honor at a project he had directed in Texas. As our trip to San Antonio neared, Julia began to see the picture—in nightmares. After one such dream, she awoke crying and confessed, "I've been pretending Dad was on a business trip."

As Julia sobbed in my arms, I longed to give Chris a high-five (as opposed to shaking my fist at him while teaching Lee to drive). Our daughter, the one who took her own sweet time with milestones— teething, talking, reading—was finally grieving.

That was the moment I realized how perverse motherhood is. My children have had five mothers between them. Each did what she believed was best for her child, no matter anyone's pain. Knowing that grief delayed was grief denied, I prayed Julia would cry rivers.

Once Julia was no longer awaiting her dad's return, she asked to take a trip of her own: to Korea. To my surprise, Lee was willing, and I was when-do-we-leave ready, having frequently talked about the journey with Chris before he became ill.

The morning we convened with nine other adoptive families at Dulles International Airport, the first person I spied was the mother of Julia's erstwhile fellow flier. I had not spoken to Lyndi in fifteen years, yet I felt instantly at ease. One would have thought that we were long-lost friends, or at least that we knew each other.

There was also another widow in the group, with a son and a daughter, who was Julia's age. What were the chances of that? For the next two weeks, we warmed the empty seats next to each other during ten-hour forays on the bus, trading tales about the indecencies of death and the insolence of life, which had all the compassion of a traffic cop shouting, "Move along!"

In Seoul, we began at the agency that had placed most of the children. Touring the infant ward of Eastern Social Welfare Society, where babies in bassinettes slumbered in limbo, the adoptees longed to adopt themselves. Afterward, each child had a "file review." When Julia's caseworker improbably revealed the names of her birth parents, I was so taken by surprise, I found myself scrambling for pen and paper.

The next day, during a question-and-answer session at Esther's Home for unwed mothers, Lee found himself scrambling for forgiveness.

When we convened in the shelter's small dining hall, a dozen young women were already seated around a long table, half with their backs to the room, one struggling against tears. The home's director briefly introduced each mother, and then the wireless microphone was passed to us. One by one, we delicately probed their feelings or praised them for their courage in making their decisions and in facing us.

One adoptive mother pleaded for each birth mother to convey a photograph of herself with her infant. A thirteen-year-old boy, with the face and grace of a bodhisattva, reassured the women that he thought about his birth mother every day. When I asked if in-country placement would make their decisions any easier, one mother replied that she preferred international adoption, for it offered her a chance of later finding her child. But another tersely stated that she had not decided on relinquishment, and then she questioned why people would adopt babies they abused, as reported in the news. Several parents replied that, loving our children as much as we do, we could only wonder how that happened, too.

Without waiting for the mike, Lee declared, "I've been angry with my birth mother all these years." His tone and impolitic slouch said as much.

I clenched. The young women riveted their eyes on him, awaiting a translation.

"But now," he continued, "after meeting all of you, I hope I can someday find her."

Lee's birthplace in Masan was only an hour's drive from Pusan, where we were booked for two nights. Julia's, however, was at Kangnung on the northeast coast, which required spending a night on our own. As I second-guessed my mission, Julia made the decision easy. She had no interest in leaving the group—or, to be precise, a certain someone in the group. He loved manga, too, and lived fifteen minutes from us in Maryland. Faced with choosing between the past and the future, she chose the future. So did I.

Having spent the cost of a Hyundai Accent getting to South Korea, I didn't blink at the quote of 90,000 won (about $100) for roundtrip cab fare to Masan. The morning our group left to tour the fish market on Pusan's docks, my children and I hopped a taxi in pursuit of Fatima Hospital. Riding shotgun, as she phrased it, was the tour's translator, Susan, a native Korean who was a student at Wellesley College.

Halfway there, the driver pulled into a rest stop and treated us to a bag of Korean donuts. Back on the highway, he seemed eager to join our freewheeling discussion, and Susan was happy to translate. Ever curious about prejudice, I asked at one point if Korean parents would more easily embrace a Chinese or a Japanese son-in-law. He and Susan differed, but I laughed when they agreed that a Caucasian would be their last choice, given the risk of being "whitewashed."

We arrived to discover that the hospital had been replaced by a mental health and geriatric care center. Perusing Lee's documents, Susan and the receptionist also deduced that he wasn't born at Fatima but was transferred there after his birth, due to prematurity. The news in no way lessened my desire to see where my son had spent his first month. Unfortunately, apart from the lobby, a back stairway was the only unrestricted area.

As we wound single-file up the narrow, spiral steps, I pretended I was Lee's birth mother on the day he arrived. Never having given birth or had parents who rejected my child, I could not imagine her state of mind. And that was undoubtedly a mercy.

On each landing, we met with a door blocking further access. By the third floor, I was ready to turn back—especially because through that door's porthole the view was of floor-to-ceiling bars. Only after I reversed our procession did I notice that the driver had joined Lee's birthplace tour, and he was now in the lead. One would have thought that they were long-lost kin, or at least that they knew each other.

That afternoon, back in Pusan, I went out alone to explore the city to practice finding my way without Chris. I returned with newfound confidence— only to get lost between the subway stop and the hotel. Map in hand, I approached several pedestrians, but no one could pinpoint my location. Finally, I flagged down two young men. As they debated between themselves in Korean, another voice called out. I turned to see a slight, middle-aged man waving at us from a block away.

"I know him!" I exclaimed to my would-be guides, who looked more lost than ever.

The driver churned the air with an arm, as if reeling me into his cab—the cab I had ridden to Masan. "Come!" he insisted, though he didn't speak English. "Service," he added, "service!"

Laughing at our improbable reunion, I obliged. Don't ask me how, but we managed to communicate as he drove me to my hotel. And don't ask me why, but he suddenly meant the world to me. When he refused his fare, I realized *service* is Korean for *gratis*.

"What are the chances of that?" I later said to Susan. "In a city of more than three million people?"

"Oooh," she crooned, turning serious. "In Korea, when people find each other again like that, we call it . . . " and she said a Korean word that I later learned means *destiny*.

I call it hide-and-seek. The game of going missing. The game of finding people who find you.

On the flight home, Julia sat across the aisle from the boy who had traveled "home" with her fifteen years before. Beside her sat her new companion. He's been keeping her company ever since.

—Gaye Brown

A version of this story was first published in Adoptive Families *magazine, November/December 2008.*

What Matters Most

"Mom, where did we live when you borned me?"

Marty's question floated to the kitchen sink, where I stood washing dishes while my children lingered around the dinner table. His words hurled me four years into the past, to the peaceful summer morning when I'd first heard them.

Busily mending little boys' shirts, I'd been lulled into motherly contentment by the sounds of my three sons playing outside the bedroom window. Protected from the morning sun, that section of the yard was the ideal place to haul dirt in their Tonka trucks. Their voices provided all the sound effects as make-believe engines roared and Matchbox cars sped up and down dirt hills. My contentment was soon disturbed by a shift in their conversation.

"Come on, Marty, you drink it," Dale coaxed, pointing to the puddle of water fed by drippings from the evaporative water cooler wedged into the top of the bedroom window.

"No, I don't want to. Drink it yourself," Marty said.

Four-year-old Mark agreed, "Yeah, Dale, you drink it. Me and Marty will if you will."

"You do it first, Marty. You like dirty water," Dale cajoled.

Uh-oh, I thought, *it's about time to interfere in this little game.*

"Not since I lived with you, I don't."

The weight of Marty's words sounded too heavy for his little, almost five-year-old body to carry. I dropped my sewing and reached the window in two quick strides. *Oh God*, I prayed, *how do I handle this?*

Gentle words forced their way through my rapidly tightening throat. "Marty, what do you mean? Haven't you almost always lived with us?"

"Not when I was borned I didn't." Though he spoke slowly and softly, his words echoed sharply with pain, as if he were crying out from the bottom of a deep stonewalled well. Head bowed, fingers sifting dirt, my son sat with legs splayed out from his hips in the endearing loose-jointed position that belonged strictly to him. Dale and Mark sat cross-legged on either side, silenced by words they didn't understand but understanding that their brother was hurting.

"Marty, come here, will you?" My words felt like pebbles pushing their way through a straw.

Marty rose to his feet, and eyes on the ground, he walked slowly into the house. I sat down in my sewing chair and waited with my heart clenched into a tight ball. His blue eyes were stagnant pools, lifeless and dull, when he entered the bedroom. I lifted him onto my lap and nestled his head against my neck.

Two days earlier a church member who owned a small farm ten miles away had come with fresh vegetables for us. We were standing near the door chatting when Marty came into the room. As she watched him playing quietly with his Matchbox cars on the end table in the corner, she lowered her voice and asked, "Is he the adopted one?"

Caught off guard, I glanced quickly at Marty and nodded silently. He looked up at her question. His left eye had a tendency to roll upward when he was stressed or ill, and now his pupil was barely visible. With a sudden surge of temper, he swept his cars off the table. Hurriedly, I bid our visitor goodbye and rushed to kneel beside my son. Calmly, I helped him gather his scattered cars and soothed him with playful words. For the first time, I wondered if the word "adopted" made him feel different. I felt a sudden rush of anger at the experts whose professional knowledge I had blindly trusted. Perhaps we shouldn't have been so open and honest about his adoption, as they'd suggested.

Considering the circumstances, though, remaining silent would have been difficult.

It had been four years since we'd received the call that my husband's sister was in the hospital, terminally ill with cancer. Within two hours, we were on our way to California. Five hours later, at my in-laws' home, I found Marty in a bedroom alone, standing in his crib, his left eye turned upward. He was not yet eleven months old, just beginning to walk. My sister-in-law's round-faced, tow-headed baby was a heartbreaking picture of confusion and sadness, unable to comprehend what had happened to his secure world of Mommy and Daddy and six older brothers and sisters.

For six weeks, Marty had been shuffled from one caregiver to another, his mother too sick to take care of him. Now, he was in the home of weary, elderly grandparents, who were also trying to cope with their daughter's dying. How could I return to my own home and leave this confused little boy? A few hours later, at his mother's bedside, I asked her permission to take her baby home with us.

"I can't take care of him," she brokenly answered and nodded her permission. Tears rolled down her cheeks as she grasped my hand.

Two nights later, traveling home to Arizona through the desert darkness, my husband and I discussed our new responsibility. Marty lay asleep in the seat between us, his head on my lap, his hand curled around my fingers. Our own baby, not yet five months old, was asleep within my other arm. The back seat was filled with Marty's dismantled crib, covered with blankets to make a bed for our almost five-year-old son and six-year-old daughter. How would the congregation of the small church where my husband was pastor react to the extra demands on our time, energy, and finances created by another baby only six months older than our own?

The next Sunday morning, I sat in church with Marty in my arms and baby Mark asleep in the church nursery, silently rejoicing as our congregation enfolded a confused little boy into our church family.

I loved the afternoon hours spent in the rocking chair singing my babies to sleep, one nestled in each arm, their legs intertwined. Marty and Mark were as close as only near-twins can be, sharing everything from diapers and bottles to toys, chickenpox, and measles. Seven months later, Marty's mother died. She was buried on my birthday. Her gift to me was her final request that we raise her baby. By then, he was part of our family, a happy little toddler. We waited several months before asking his grief-stricken father, overwhelmed with the care of his six older children, for permission to adopt Marty. A year later, Marty's adoption became final.

The six-months age difference between our two babies was often cause for questions by people unaware of the situation. Clearly, hiding his adoption wasn't possible. Then came that afternoon when I saw my adopted son's face turn bleak and angry at my visitor's question. I needed time to think, time to consider how to handle this new situation.

But two days later, with Marty hurting and cuddled in my arms, I'd come face-to-face with it. What could I do to bring healing to my little boy? His cry, "Not when I was borned, I didn't," enclosed the two of us in a private world belonging only to us. Love for this child overwhelmed me with its intensity. His pain was my pain.

"Marty, does that word *adopted* make you feel different from your brothers and sister?"

"Yes," he whispered.

I cradled him tighter, wanting to gather every inch of his body against mine.

"Marty, you will never have to feel different again." The words were like thick mush in my mouth.

It was a promise I meant to keep. The word *adopted* would no longer be part of our vocabulary.

My son and I sat quietly, holding and being held. Every fiber of my being was alive with the agonizing pain of childbirth that brings mother and child united into their world. The pain brought my other three children to me through the passage of my body's birth canal. This pain brought Marty to me through the passage of my heart. Both were part of my flesh, one no less than the other.

"Mom, where did we live when you borned me?"

I turned from the kitchen sink and looked at my four children waiting in curious anticipation. Their conversation had pleasantly arrived at a discussion about their various places of birth. The lump in my throat melted into a cascade of joy for what the passing years had given us since I'd made that promise to Marty. He no longer felt different. In fact, he no longer remembered he was adopted.

"Let's see, Marty," I thoughtfully considered his question, "your sister and Mark were born in the same hospital in Arizona, and you and Dale were born in hospitals in California."

The children were content with that simple answer. I turned back to the sink, thankful that my child no longer lived with pain. The day would come when I would need to tell him about his adoption, but next time it would be told in a way he could understand. It would be told when the time was right.

Several weeks later, comments made by their playmates about the six-month age difference between Mark and Marty came to my attention. The right time had arrived. And so, after a summer's day of play, I called my son in for his bedtime bath. Kneeling beside him, I soaped and scrubbed his back while I told the story of his mother's illness and death, and how glad we were that she had chosen me to take her place. I promised him it would make no difference to Mark, just as it made no difference to his older brother and sister. Afterward, in his pajamas, Marty went outside to the backyard as I called Mark in for his bath and repeated the story.

"They said Marty was adopted, but I didn't believe them," Mark said about their playmates.

He hurried into his pajamas and went to find his brother. I rushed to the bedroom window. My two sons were sitting on the grass side by side, their backs to the window, Mark cross-legged and Marty's legs splayed out from his hips in that uniquely-his-own way. I couldn't hear their words, but their closeness and posture told it all: It makes no difference. We're brothers, and nothing else matters.

—Marian Webster

That Saucy One

"Marjorie, please, you must answer me!"

I stood facing my seventy-five-year-old sister, who sat silently, shrinking in her seat, as I confronted her. My surprise visit had at first pleased her, but my question had shocked her. Her eyes brimmed with tears, her lips quivered, and finally she spoke.

"I promised Mother and Father I would never tell you, and even though they're gone, I feel I am betraying their trust."

So it was true! Now what?

My sister, Marjorie Mae, and I, Betty Marilyn Jean, were raised and educated in Toronto, Ontario, Canada, by our loving parents, Arthur and Celina Hetherington. In 1946, at the age of twenty, I married Karl Forrest, and as Betty Forrest raised two fine sons, but sadly, I lost Karl to a heart attack when I was in my forties.

A few years later, I remarried and became Betty Hard. My new partner, Gord, and I moved north and began enjoying life on two acres of farmland in central Ontario. The location was ideal, because my sister Marjorie lived just a half-hour drive away. When our parents passed, Marjorie and I were the last of our line, and we grew closer. Then, during the summer of my sixty-fifth year, I received a surprising and perplexing telephone call.

The caller identified herself as Marian McIsaac, a name unfamiliar to me. She told me that she was my sister. I thought it was a prank call and said so, but then she posed a question about my birthplace and confirmed a fact that no one but I knew.

I paused to digest what she had said and replied quite calmly, "Well, that's interesting, but the only family I have ever known is my Mom and Dad Hetherington and my big sister, Marjorie."

She acknowledged my skepticism but implored me to ask Marjorie to verify what she had told me. She closed by giving me her telephone number, hoping I would call back. My reply to her was noncommittal, but I knew my next call would be to Marjorie.

Gord, however, dissuaded me. This would be better done in person, he felt, and he suggested we pay Marjorie a visit that very day.

So there I stood, confronting my sister, struggling to unravel a life-altering mystery.

I resumed my interrogation. Though my heart was pounding, I lowered my voice and softened my tone a little as I coaxed her. "Marjorie, the secret is out, and I would rather learn the truth from you than from a stranger."

Marjorie pointed at the tea pot, and I poured her another cup. She added milk and began to stir, and as the spoon clinked on china, she haltingly began to tell me the tale of "that saucy one."

"In 1929, Mum, Dad, and I were living on Barton Avenue in Toronto. They wanted another child, and I wanted a little sister, but Mum was unable to conceive, so they decided to adopt. Mum had relatives in Orillia, and they told her of a family that had fallen on hard times. The mother had died, and the father was struggling to raise five young children.

"In those days, adoption was largely a personal, rather than a legal, matter, so Mum, Dad, and I drove to Orillia to meet the family and to pick out a child. When we arrived, four of the children were playing in the yard, and their father, a Mr. Shakell, greeted us and invited us into the sitting room.

"The baby girl was there asleep in a crib. I sat close to Mum, holding her hand and trying not to fidget. It was hard, because my heart was racing and my stomach was squirming at the thought of getting an instant sister."

At this point in the story, Marjorie's eyes began to well. She paused in the telling, took a long sip from her tea cup, and then began again.

"Dad and Mr. Shakell were discussing the adoption when a red-haired little girl in grubby play clothes burst into the room and interrupted Mr. Shakell by giving him a light kick in the shins and exclaiming in a saucy voice, 'I want some ice cream!'

"After admonishing her, the father introduced her as his three-year-old daughter, Doris. Dad spoke up and suggested that he take all the children to the corner store for ice cream. Mr. Shakell stayed with the baby, and off we went to get our treat.

"Doris led the way, advising us of the best flavors and of her favorites and imploring us to hurry. We all got cones, and on the walk back, I spoke to Mum and told her that I liked the saucy one with the red hair and suggested that we pick her.

"Dad had been observing the children carefully, and now he spoke up, agreeing with me, Mum made it unanimous. Saucy little Doris was to be adopted into the Hetherington family.

"You are Doris.

"Back at the house, Mr. Shakell was a little surprised by our choice but apparently unfazed. He confirmed that Doris could be the child to go. You were taken off to change clothes and reappeared a short time later with your face scrubbed, hair combed, and carrying a small suitcase.

"We said goodbye, and without a hug or a wave, you walked with us to the car and took your place beside me, your new sister, in the back seat.

"During the trip back to Toronto, I asked if you really liked the name Doris. Apparently, you really didn't care, so it was agreed that you would be given a new name. Betty Boop was popular at that time, and Dad wanted Betty. Mom preferred Marilyn, and my favorite was Jean. So, on that day, you became Betty Marilyn Jean Hetherington.

"When we arrived home, we took you on a tour and showed you your new room. You couldn't believe you had a whole room just for yourself!

"We sat down to tea, milk, and cookies, and Mum and Dad explained that you would be staying with us forever. You finally began to understand and ran upstairs to your room and sat looking out the window. I came and sat near you, and I remember that, between bouts of tears, you kept telling me over and over again that you were going to watch out the window for your real dad to come and get you. Of course, he didn't."

Marjorie's tea cup began to shake in her hands, and she paused, raising it to her lips. She sipped, closed here eyes, and sat silent for what seemed an eternity. When she reopened them, they sparkled with tears, but she continued.

"Mum and Dad assured me that you would eventually forget and made me promise that I would never tell you. And as time passed, you lost all memory of your former life, and to be honest, I did too. I never broke that promise . . . until today. Yes, you were adopted. You were born Doris Shakell in Orillia."

I moved to sit beside Marjorie and put my arm around her. "Thank you!" I said and hugged her hard. "It was not your fault, and you were the best big sister a girl could ever have!"

Then we both cried. When order was restored, we felt much better. Marjorie encouraged me to call Marian and try to reconnect with my birth family.

It took me a few days to get up the courage to make the call, and I must admit that, even though I had a stiff drink beforehand, my hand was shaking as I dialed the number.

Marian answered, and when she heard it was me, the warm tone of her greeting got us off to a good start. I told her what Marjorie had told me, and she confirmed what she knew. Then I asked the big question: why had she waited so long to contact me?

Marian explained that my adoptive father had asked our birth father not to contact me ever again; in turn, my birth father told my siblings to follow suit. However, as she grew older, Marian decided to track me down. She was able to do so and followed the course of my life for many years and then finally decided I should be told of my heritage. I learned she was three years older than me and that my younger sister, Fern (the baby in the crib), was currently visiting from British Columbia. They wanted to see me in person, so we planned to meet. We chose what turned out to be a perfect setting, a restaurant in our old hometown of Orillia.

On the day of my trip to meet my mystery family, Gord and I arrived at the restaurant early and chose a table facing the door, so we could watch for them. Soon two women entered, and as they approached our table, I could tell we were related. After some tentative hugs, the ice was broken and time just flew by. When we finished our lunch, we decided to drive to a waterfront park, and on the way we passed the home where I was born. I got goose bumps!

We sat at a picnic table on the shore of Lake Couchiching and spent a happy afternoon getting to know one another. My birth father had, of course, passed on, but I did learn that I had two older brothers, both now deceased, and it was confirmed that our mother had died from complications when giving birth to Fern. Sadly, her passing had left her husband with five children to raise with only the help of his mother. Grandma cared for Fern, Marian, and me, while Dad was coping with our brothers and working full-time to keep us all fed and clothed. But it was just too much, so after some discussion, they decided that perhaps one girl could be adopted out. And, as I now knew, I was, by default, the one to go.

Marian and I exchanged addresses and telephone numbers and promised to send photos and keep in touch—and we have.

My sister Marjorie has since passed away, so my last ties with my adoptive family are gone. My "new" big sister, Marian, and I stay in touch often, and this summer I am traveling across Canada to visit my younger sister, Fern, in British Columbia.

When my second husband, Gord, passed away, I moved to—of all places—Orillia to be near my son John, who, coincidently enough, had settled and raised his family there. He and they are enjoying getting to know their new aunts, nieces, and nephews and their children. Oh how I wish I could have met my brothers and introduced my sons to their Orillia grandfather!

I am now eighty-one, and over the intervening years I have often pondered my dual heritages. *Why did my family not want to tell me of my adoption? Would my life have been different if I had known earlier that I was born Doris Shakell in Orillia? Would I have sought out my birth family? Would they have welcomed or shunned me? How would my sons have reacted, then, to having a whole new family in their lives?*

I don't know the answers to those questions. What I do know is that I am very lucky that a saucy little girl was chosen to begin a new life with a wonderful family, and that I now have my birth family back in my life.

—Betty Hard

The Woman with the Long, Auburn Hair

"Congratulations! You have a new daughter. She's a doll. Be at the agency at ten tomorrow."

Peter, the adoption worker, had just called with the news we'd been anxiously awaiting. Bernie and I jumped up, wrapping our arms around each other in a long hug, excited that we would soon be parents for the second time.

Our three-year-old son, David, picked up on our enthusiasm. "I'm a big brother. She be mine."

The next day, the three of us congregated in Peter's office, sitting on hard wooden chairs across from his desk. He read silently from his files, every now and then looking up to share information he thought important. "There's a minor foot issue. She's pigeon-toed; should be easy to correct. And you're a visiting nurse."

"Yes. We will make sure she's treated. Helping new moms and their babies is a big part of my job. And I've taken a leave of absence from work."

"Good. Her birth mother is a nineteen-year-old college sophomore, an Irish girl majoring in Bible studies." He read on. "She has long, auburn hair, plays the piano, and is cheerful with an outgoing personality."

I nodded and smiled, but inside I compared myself. *I'm so different. Nearly thirty and of Swiss descent, quiet and sometimes shy. No musical ability, can't even carry a tune. And my short brown hair rarely has been longer than my shoulders. How would I measure up? Could I be the mother this young woman with the long, auburn hair expected for her newborn daughter?* As I listened to Peter, these thoughts and questions circled through my mind like buzzing flies.

A loud intercom announcement broke my reverie. Peter closed the door and telephoned his assistant. "Bring in the baby."

I could only stare at the round clock on the wall and watch the black second hand move around the numbers as I listened for the assistant's footsteps. Suddenly, the door cracked open, and a heavy middle-aged woman stood at the doorway holding an infant wrapped in a pink blanket.

She put the baby in my arms. "This little darling is three weeks old today."

I stroked the baby's tufts of red hair and looked into her eyes as blue as a sun-filled summer sky. "She's beautiful," I whispered.

A warm feeling filled my body from head to toe, yet I thought about the baby's birth mother holding her newborn for the last time. I envisioned wispy tears running down her cheeks as she handed the infant to the hospital's social worker. Did she doubt her decision, worried the adoptive parents wouldn't love her angelic baby enough? I wished I could tell her how grateful I felt and that I would do my best to mother her child.

We left the adoption agency with our daughter dressed in a yellow sleeper with matching bunting. The baby clung to my shoulder as I walked down the building's steep concrete steps. I hated to put her in the car seat for the ride home, not wanting to be even that far from her for that short period.

Minutes after we pulled into our driveway, family and friends arrived to congratulate us. Neighbors brought food to add to the celebration. My earlier feelings of uncertainty and thoughts of the woman with the long, auburn hair were replaced by excitement and the practical issues of parenting a second child. We named our daughter Debbie. From the start, she was a sociable and contented baby and adapted to our busy household.

Even though I was following the physician's orders for daily ankle stretching, her feet continued to turn inward. I contacted the pediatrician again.

"We'll need to try braces, full-length plastic ones. Keep them on both legs for twenty-three hours every day."

"Twenty-three hours? It sounds so cruel." I wiped my eyes with a tissue.

"Right. For six weeks. Bring her back. We'll know by then if we need to operate."

Operate? This was much more serious than I'd thought.

Debbie screamed when I first applied the braces, and I wondered what the woman with the long, auburn hair would think if she heard her child crying like this. Would she consider me uncaring? Was I doing the right thing to follow the doctor's orders so diligently, keeping the braces on for twenty-three hours a day? Or should I ease into it?

Just as the doctor had ordered, I left the braces in place but carried Debbie on my hip to comfort her. In a week, she was laughing, lifting her legs, and scooting up in her crib, not seeming to mind the braces.

It was a different story for me. The days inside the house grew long, and time passed slowly. I worried the braces wouldn't work and Debbie would need surgery. I wished I could tell the woman with the long, auburn hair that dealing with the foot problem was difficult, but I still loved her baby.

Two months later, the doctor told us, "She's responding well. She won't need an operation."

I began to relax and forget about the woman with the long, auburn hair.

My husband and I read bedtime stories about adopted children to our little girl. When she was six, she told her grandparents, "I'm adopted. I grew in another woman's tummy." Imagine my surprise when a neighbor laughingly commented that Debbie had said, "Mommy and Daddy bought me from Sears. They ordered me from a catalog and picked me because I had red hair the same as my other mother."

Debbie kept the auburn-colored hair like her biological mother. She had a quick fiery temper when she was upset but grew up as a normal kid, playing a lot with her friends and joining the track team in middle school. She sped around the asphalt track, her feet as straight as an arrow shot into a bull's-eye, so different from when we'd first brought her home from the adoption agency.

When Debbie was sixteen, she started working weekends at Loehmann's, the women's clothing outlet. Clothes and fashion fascinated her, and she spent most of her paycheck buying outfits with her store discount.

In her senior year of high school, arguments about clothes spending threatened our relationship. When Debbie came home one afternoon with another designer sweater, I grabbed the bag from her hand and said, "You're taking this back to the store now."

"My real mother would buy them for me," she screamed. "She'd buy me anything I wanted."

I yelled back, "You don't take care of your clothes. They're all over the floor."

"It's my room. I wish I could live with my other mother. She has prettier hair than you do, anyhow."

Whoa, I thought. *What kind of mother am I, anyway?* The woman with the long, auburn hair had come back into my life.

I ran my fingers through my short hair. "When you graduate from high school, I'll help you find her," I stammered in a raspy voice, wondering if I would ever really be able to do that.

"I want to find her myself. I don't want you involved."

"Okay." I felt the blood drain from my face as I backed out of the room, unsure if Debbie still loved me. I took a deep breath, wishing I'd never told her the color of her mother's hair.

At times the tension between us became chaotic. Quiescent periods were interspersed with arguments about weekend parties, household chores, curfews, and homework assignments. I thought again of the woman with the long, auburn hair. There was no way she could handle this rebellion any better than I was.

I was so sure of myself, certain that I was right in what I expected from my daughter, that I really didn't try to understand her feelings. A Mother's Day card Debbie gave me when she was seventeen included a hand-written poem scrawled in pencil on a sheet of yellow, lined notebook paper. The poem jolted me into looking at our relationship differently.

Sometimes, I am angry
And can't stand your ways
It seems all we've been doing
Is fighting these days

You don't understand me
We can't even talk
I can't figure you out
Unless we scream and shout
Why is it we've grown
So far, far apart?
When I think of it all
It crushes my heart

We're not living up
To the standards we've set

For mother and daughter
We're not there quite yet

I want you to know
That I love you a lot
And wish we could get
Along like we ought

I'm willing to try
To make things go right
And, Mom, I still think
You're out of sight.

HAPPY MOTHER'S DAY

I love you, Debbie

The poem brought tears to my eyes, and I rocked her in a bear hug, whispering, "I'll do my best to make it right, too."

I vowed to better understand my daughter and to be more attentive. We started going out to lunch once a week, where Debbie began sharing her thoughts and experiences more honestly, and I slowly learned to keep quiet and listen.

Some months later, Debbie announced, "I don't want to see my other mother now. I'll wait until later, when I'm older."

I took a deep breath, feeling more secure about the love between us. The woman with the long, auburn hair receded from my mind—until Debbie's eighteenth birthday. Then, I thought about her again. How does she feel on this special day? Could she envision Debbie as an adult or did she still see her as a child?

One afternoon that summer, Debbie and I drove to Michigan State University, where her brother was a college senior. The two of us waited for him on a bench in a small park-like alcove. From out of nowhere, a thin, thirty-something woman with shoulder-length auburn hair walked into the garden. She seemed lost, wandering back and forth and glancing in our direction once in a while. The thought of her being the woman with the long, auburn hair zigzagged through my mind like a lightening bolt on the ocean's horizon. Impossible, I thought. We're too far away from home. Yet the connection felt strong, strange, and surreal, and the resemblance between the two women was startling.

Did Debbie notice anything? I looked at her and she said, "You know, Mom, that lady has the exact same hair color as me."

I took a deep breath. "Yes, there is something familiar about her."

"Should we talk to her?" she asked.

"Do you want to?"

Debbie looked confused and shook her head. "I don't know."

Soon the woman walked away just as quietly as she'd come.

Debbie glanced up at me and smiled. "I'm glad you let me quit piano lessons after a year. I only wanted to take them because of my other mother."

"She'll always be part of you," I said.

"But you're always the best mom in the world."

I hugged her and knew we'd come full circle.

Debbie has had the best of both worlds—traits of both her biological mother and me. She doesn't play the piano but loves music, dancing, and yoga. She has little curiosity for my favorite pasttimes of reading, writing, and gardening. Yet, she has my compelling desire to analyze relationships and spiritual ideas.

The afternoon that Debbie married Dan, I pictured this unique woman I'd never met sitting in a front pew of the church watching her daughter walk down the aisle in her bridal gown. Was she sad to have missed all the major milestones of her child's life, especially this day? Whether or not she was the woman in the park is not important. I'm forever grateful to her. How brave she was to trust another couple to raise her first-born child. Her willingness to give us her baby has invisibly connected our family to her forever.

Maybe someday Debbie will search for her biological mother, and I will finally meet the woman with the long, auburn hair and be able to share snippets of my motherhood experiences with her. Until then, I wish I at least knew her name. Any personal detail about the woman with the long, auburn hair would make her now ethereal image real and tangible. Like the clasp of a necklace hooking the two ends together, a friendship with her would complete our family circle and connect the missing pieces of lost time.

—Lois Gerber

Russian Lullaby

A young couple, overloaded with unaccustomed diaper bags, strollers, and two squirming toddlers, made their way down the aisle of the full airplane to the last row of seats in coach. Jeff and Julie offered apologies to various passengers after a teddy bear dropped onto someone's laptop, a blankie snagged on an armrest, and heads were bumped with their massive bags. "Sorry, so sorry, please excuse us," they repeated.

The group of four collapsed into their seats with a collective, exhausted sigh. It had been a harrowing journey, begun more than a year and a half earlier when Jeff and Julie VanBaale had taken the leap and applied to adopt after years of disappointments in their quest to have a family. Their little boys, just shy of their second birthdays, had been adopted from the same orphanage in Russia and were now brothers. The couple's dream of bringing children into their home was close to fulfillment. The last hurdle they faced was the long, cross-Atlantic flight back to the United States. Already, it was going badly, and they weren't even airborne.

During their last day in Moscow, while packing suitcases and finalizing paperwork, the boys had come down with ear infections, and Julie had fallen ill with a case of the flu and a 103° fever. The stress of the trip and hotel living had taken its toll on them all. As the plane awaited its turn on the runway for takeoff, the boys began to fuss and whine, tugging at their ears, and Julie broke into a coughing fit that left her breathless. Jeff finally managed to shush Ryan to sleep and tucked him into his seat while Julie took a strong flu medication herself and was mercifully out cold by the time the plane barreled down the runway.

But just as the plane reached cruising altitude, Jake began to wail inconsolably, the cabin pressure causing excruciating pain in his infected ear. He writhed around in his father's arms, crying out broken words and phrases. *"Povrezdenje! Uxo!"*

Jeff jostled the boy on his lap and attempted to dig through the diaper bag for their translation dictionary but came up empty-handed.

"P-o-v-a-r," he struggled to repeat. "I, I don't know what you're saying," he shook his head helplessly. "I don't understand."

But the little boy only cried harder.

Passengers around them began to squirm with annoyance and to shoot looks of irritation. For what felt like hours, Jeff desperately tried everything he could think of—baby Tylenol, treats, rocking, warm cloths over his son's ears—but nothing worked. He was a novice. As Jeff cradled this virtual stranger in his arms, tears streaming down the little boy's red, swollen face, a terrible feeling of doubt washed over him. This was so much harder than he'd thought it would be. What if they'd made a terrible mistake?

At that moment, an elderly woman wearing a colorful kerchief over her hair appeared next to his seat. "I hold?" she asked, her words slow and deliberate with a thick accent.

Surprised, Jeff hesitated and drew his son closer to his chest. "Oh, no thank you. He just doesn't feel well."

She pointed to the side of Jake's head. "His bad ear. I rock baby. You rest."

He looked up into the old woman's weathered face again, taking in her kind eyes, her outstretched arms. Exhausted and near tears himself, he handed his son over to her.

The woman cradled Jake's head against her shoulder, stroking his back and neck, and started to softly sing next to his ear.

"Bai, bai, bai, bai
Bayu, detusku, mayu!
Shta na gorki, na gorye,
O visyennei, o porye."

"Bai, bai, bai, bai
Bayu, orchid, little dear!
On the hillside in the spring,
Birds of heaven sweetly sing."

At first, Jake whimpered and fought her embrace, but as Jeff watched, the little boy began to relax at the sound of familiar words he understood. The woman continued to sing the lullaby, swaying back and forth, stroking the damp tendrils of hair at the nape of his neck. After a few moments, Jake exhaled one last, unhappy breath as his heavy eyelids drifted shut. He'd settled down enough for the medicine to finally give him relief. The woman nodded to Jeff, gesturing for him to sit back, and started walking up and down the aisle with Jake in her arms.

Julie awoke then and looked around, rubbing her eyes. "Where's Jake?

Jeff pointed to the woman, still walking and singing just a few feet away.

"Is he alright?" she asked.

Jeff patted his wife's hand. "Yeah, he is. It's okay. Go back to sleep."

After a few minutes more, Jeff reclined his own seat and gratefully closed his eyes.

Before they landed in New York to change planes, the woman handed Jake, now rested and calm, back to Jeff. He and Julie thanked her profusely, trying to offer her several gestures of appreciation, but she only smiled and waved them away. When they disembarked the plane, she disappeared into the crowd and they never saw her again.

At last, they reached their final destination on a cool spring evening in Iowa and were greeted at the gate by a mass of relatives and friends eagerly waiting to celebrate their arrival. It had been the most difficult and stressful journey of their lives, nothing like what they had always imagined. But they were home. And as they trudged down the jet way, the four of them hand-in-hand, a family at last, Jeff realized they had learned their first lessons as parents. Sometimes there will be people in your child's life who can give them things you cannot. And, maybe more important, life doesn't always have to be perfect to be wonderful.

—*Kali VanBaale*

Black and White

"Hi there. That's my daughter's," I tell the small boy who's picked up Deja's scooter. "It's probably okay if you ride it, but maybe you should ask first. She's over there in the butterfly shirt."

I've come to the neighborhood playground with three-year-old Oliver and my seven-year-old daughter, Deja. The late afternoon sun is beginning to cast long shadows, yet kids' voices still fill the air. I catch sentences, "Brianna don't know how to swing yet," and "Gimme more of them chips; you ate, like, all of them."

Deja had abandoned her Razor Scooter on the paved path the moment we'd entered the fenced-in playground. Now she climbs high onto the wooden train while other children play and jump nearby.

Blond-haired Oliver had taken hesitant steps to the slide while I offered encouragement and then went down while keeping an eye on me. I'm a single parent, and sometimes things are tight, so I was babysitting him.

He and I are the only white people at the playground.

The child on Deja's scooter looks at me blankly. So I call, "Deja, is it okay if this little guy rides your scooter?" She nods her head.

It's another boy, around eight, skin the color of my morning coffee with cream, who first regards my daughter and me quizzically, then asks the inevitable question—one we've heard before, but not in a while. "That's your mom?"

I'm immediately attuned to my daughter's body language. Lately she's becoming more self-conscious and cares what kind of impression she makes. Even though I know how she'll respond, my own image-conscious radar revs up instantly. But when she answers the boy's question with a simple, "Yeah," there's no need for explanation, even though her voice sounds flat. I'm relieved that there's no embarrassed shrug of the shoulders or downcast eyes.

Deja's skin color is about the same color as the boy's, and her braids are ones I finally finished as she was falling asleep in my bed last night.

I'd always wanted a daughter. When Deja came to my home as a foster child, before she'd learned her

ABCs, bright but neglected, I fell in love so quickly that I couldn't *not* adopt her.

Now, a photo album holds a handful of pre-adoption pictures that our adoption worker was able to obtain: baby Deja and her parents at someone's graduation, at the zoo, and in a crib with ruffles and mobiles. In all the photos, her birth parents are looking into the camera and smiling, and it seems apparent that Deja began life as a loved child—until the lure of drugs tore her family apart.

Deja has told me that before I adopted her, she and her mom lived in the back of a car parked near a Laundromat, or "laundry-mat," as she says. She's also said that she once lived on a horse farm in Ireland, but I don't believe that one. Sometimes, when we're reading, she takes strands of my long hair to put in her mouth, and I don't tell her to stop.

Deja and I don't know many other black kids with white moms. The boy regarding us with his eyes squinty apparently doesn't either, for after a pause he asks, "How can she be your mom?"

Here, my own need for acceptance, to be understood, rises to the surface, and I ask him, "Do you know what adoption is?"

"She adopted?" But instead of waiting for an answer, he hops from the train and runs off even as I'm deciding what to say next.

Now the scooter lies on the concrete again, so I offer Oliver a ride, and as I'm pushing him, I assume how natural for anyone looking to assume he's my son. No questions will be asked of us. But later, heading home with Oliver and Deja, I'll be watchful; I'll know that even in the racial melting pot of the San Francisco Bay Area, people going by may speculate about our family configuration, like the boy on the playground did. Most people never say anything, yet I feel their eyes, while others voice their opinions out loud—some with rancor or ignorance; others, interested. Either way, they know, and I do, too, that transracial families like ours will probably never get represented on prime-time television.

I can't help but wonder whether there will come a time when Deja not only asks that I drop her a block from school but also whether she'll lose her sense of pride in our family simply because we're different. I'm acutely aware that I'll never know what it is to be a black female in America and that, no matter how much I surround my daughter with others from her culture, no matter how many black dolls she has or how many African-American history books she reads, I'll always question whether I'm doing enough. I'll wonder if the double-whammy of being adopted and being adopted by a single, white parent will wreak emotional havoc on her down the road.

At least, for now, I feel almost smug thinking how I've crossed a racial barrier that few people are willing to cross. And I can only hope that Deja will continue to feel sufficiently nurtured by the bond we share to face whatever challenges lie ahead.

A few minutes later, she says, "Look, Mom," and jumps off the train, landing gracefully in the sand, her smile triumphant. "Do you want to see me again?"

"You go, girl," I reply—a phrase I'd never uttered to anyone before I had a black daughter.

The sun is sinking, and it's getting nippier. Buttoning my sweater, I call to Deja, "You want to give Oliver a ride home on your scooter soon?"

"'K," she replies, and a few minutes later she's walking toward the silver scooter, smiling and breathing fast as I help Oliver balance so he can ride on the scooter in front of her. Then my beautiful daughter pushes a strong leg against the sidewalk, and we head toward home, where Oliver will soon be picked up by his family, and I'll start fixing dinner for mine.

—Annie Kassof

A version of this story was first published in Fostering Families Today *magazine, March/April 2005.*

Are You Adopted?

I still remember it as if it were yesterday. It was a beautiful, crisp fall afternoon. The sun was casting a golden glow on the trees with leaves that were beginning to turn red and orange. I was on my way home from grade school, sitting in the perfect place to be the first one off the school bus. With my hand on the pole by the door, I was ready to swing onto the steps in front of Larry, who was sitting across the aisle. Larry lived down the street from me, and both being ten years old, we were enemies. Our communication was limited to pushing and shoving as we got off the bus.

Needless to say, I was completely caught off-guard when he suddenly turned to me and said, "Can I ask you a question?"

Of course, I thought he was just trying to distract me from our bus stop. So I sat closer to the edge of my seat, kept my eyes straight ahead, and answered "yes" in the most disdainful voice I could. His question, however, was a bomb waiting to explode.

"Are you adopted?" he asked.

Without thinking, I rolled my eyes and shook my head no as I thought, *Adopted? How stupid! What is he talking about?* I gave him a disgusted look and indignantly said, "No!" Then I promptly turned my attention back to the road ahead and our bus stop, which was coming into view.

My mind, however, went into overdrive. That question was really strange, even for Larry, and I wondered where in the world he could have gotten that idea. I was an only child in a close-knit family, and being adopted had never even remotely crossed my mind. Still, I could tell that he was sincere when he asked the question, and I just knew he hadn't come up with it on his own. So I turned and asked, "Who told you that?"

I was surprised when he said, "Debbie."

Finally, he had my full attention. Debbie was a girl who lived down the street from both of us. Normally, for any other subject I would have totally dismissed her comment. However, her mother and mine had been friends for many years, and we went to the same church. Maybe she knew something I didn't. So this time I turned and looked at Larry when I said, "I don't think I'm adopted, but I'll ask my mom when I get home."

When the bus stopped, Larry and I elbowed each other as we pushed our way down the steps, both of us landing on the street at about the same moment. This time, though, I didn't feel like getting in a fight. I took off down the street with the other kids.

Even though Larry's question had been a surprise, I'd forgotten about it by the time I got home. The weather was great, and I wanted to ride my bike. I ran in the house and went right to my room to change my clothes. My mom was in the kitchen working on dinner and didn't look up as I said I was going outside to play. Then I remembered my conversation with Larry. Stopping at the back door, I innocently dropped the bomb.

"Hey, Mom. Am I adopted?"

In hindsight, it really did seem like I dropped a bomb, because my mother froze. To this day I still see the paring knife suspended in mid-air over onions she had been chopping. She didn't say anything, so I impatiently asked her again. This time, she slowly moved to the sink, washed her hands, and turned around. Her face was ashen, and she looked like she wanted to cry. I had no idea why she was so upset, and I was anxious for her answer because my only thought was to go outside.

She quietly asked me why I thought I was adopted. I told her about Larry and the bus and that Debbie was the one who told him.

Taking a deep breath, Mom walked over and led me to sit beside her on the couch. This was not what I'd expected, and I certainly didn't want to have a whole conversation about this thing. A quick yes or no would have been fine.

My mom, however, saw it differently. Tearfully, she began to tell me that, yes, I was adopted. It had been her plan to tell me when I was older that she and my dad couldn't have kids of their own so they had decided to adopt and picked me as their daughter. They saw me the day I was born and brought me home when I was three days old. Expressing that they loved me with all their hearts, she sobbed and said she hoped this didn't make any difference in the way I felt about them.

I must say that, even though I could see this was clearly earth-shattering to her, none of what she said made an impact on me. I kept thinking, Okay, so I'm adopted. Big deal. As far as I was concerned, nothing had changed. All I wanted to do was to go outside and play. But my mom wanted to sit there and hug me. So I hugged her back and said I loved her, too. She was my mom and would always be my mom.

Now, as an adult, I have a better understanding of my mom's reaction. Although unfounded, her greatest fear in life was that this "truth" would change how I felt about her and my dad. Yet, as I matured, knowing about the adoption only deepened my love and appreciation for my parents. The real truth is that someone sacrificed their own feelings to give me life and then gave me a life by allowing someone else to love and raise me. Not only that, my parents accepted me completely, without reservation, and gave me unconditional love. Because I was secure in that, "adopted" has never been more than just a word to me.

It takes incredible courage to give up a child, and I believe it is a greater love when it is a choice. I will be forever thankful to my birth mother for loving me enough to give me away. I will also be eternally grateful for my parents, who loved me with all their hearts, gave me a wonderful home, and never once made me feel that I was anyone other than their child. I'm happy to say that adoption has joined us all—my birth mother, my parents, and me—in a complete circle of love.

—*Kim Johnson*

Why I Believe in Angels

Day after day, my roommates came and went, leaving with flowers, balloons, and stuffed animals, while I lingered and waited on my side of the room. Waiting for what, I didn't know. Then, one day as I sat in my hospital bed, I overheard my social worker's voice in the hallway.

I recognized my social worker's voice reply, "I know she's younger than you expected, but please go in and meet her. If you don't think it will work, just let me know."

Churning with fear and apprehension, I awaited their entrance. At seven years old, many frightening and events had led to my extended hospital stay. Abandoned, homeless, and discouraged, I felt certain I would never trust anyone again, but the moment I saw my future parents, I believed in angels.

Somewhere deep inside me, hope remained . . . and suddenly presented itself in the form of two people, Vel and Lois, my future parents. As they crossed the threshold of my sterile hospital room, they penetrated my heart and soul. Not certain if they would be interested in giving me a home, I greeted them with optimism and as if I had known them all my life. "Hi, Mom and Dad."

My parents have told me that the moment their eyes met mine and they observed my small frame looking as if I would be swallowed by the huge hospital bed, they knew they needed to take me home.

As arrangements were being made for my release from the hospital to their home, neighbors warned my new parents not to take me as their daughter, because my birth family would bring them trouble. My parents felt that whatever the rest of the family did had no bearing on their commitment to a little girl in desperate need of a loving home.

To celebrate our new family, my parents took me to my first restaurant. I was awe struck at all the food displayed on the buffet. I was shocked to see people abandoning more food on their plates than my siblings and I had shared in a week.

After we were seated at the table, I handed my mom my silverware and informed her, "I don't need this stuff." My biological family didn't gather for family meals or practice table etiquette, so I was content to eat with my fingers. My new mother may have been appalled by my primitive skills, but with grace she slid the silverware toward me and said, "We're a family, and we all use our silverware."

My biological brother and three sisters had been placed in separate foster homes. Although my mom received a lot of opposition, if it weren't for her arranging activities with my siblings, even though those visits were few and far between, we would have lost contact with each other. I am grateful for her perseverance, which led to the relationships I still have with all of my biological siblings.

I also inherited two new sisters, Gail and Dawn, which helped ease the loneliness of being separated from my biological siblings. Until then, my birth siblings had been the only four people in the world I trusted.

My personality has always been quiet and withdrawn, but my new sister Dawn, two years older than me, and I shared a kindred spunky spirit, and we quickly formed a close bond. We shared a bedroom crammed with dolls, stuffed animals, records, games, and lots of secrets, whispering, and laughing. Many times our dad arrived at our door to gently remind us that it was past our bedtime.

Before my adoption, I was a city kid who had roamed the streets without regard to safety, supervision, or rules. Suddenly, I found myself living in the quiet countryside outside of a small town, being cared for by diligent parents—and trust me, there were rules.

"I want you to see the picture Vicki drew," my teacher said to Mom at the first parent-teacher conference shortly after my adoption.

My mom was surprised and a little red-faced when the teacher displayed a picture of a mom talking, surrounded by the word "rules," written over and over.

The first time my new parents asked me, the city kid, to go to the garden and bring back green beans and mustard has become part of our favorite family lore. I was elated when I found the green beans. But I returned to the house without the mustard and said, "There's no mustard out there. I couldn't find a jar anywhere."

There were so many concepts that, at seven years old, I should have known but didn't, much to my parents' surprise. Everyday things such as riding a bike, writing my name, making a bed, and concepts of faith in God and hope in people were foreign to me. So my parents had to create ways to teach me basic concepts without damaging my already fragile sense of self-worth.

Although I had not attended enough school to pass first grade, my parents enrolled me in second grade. While the other children in my class were already reading and writing, I was learning the alphabet. With my parent's patient encouragement and tutoring, I eventually caught up with my peers. Not only that, I then went on to receive a bachelor's degree in education and to become a teacher myself.

The most important thing I learned from my new family, however, is to treat other people the way I want to be treated. They taught me this invaluable lesson without uttering a single word. Instead, I witnessed it in their living example.

Though I was adopted into the family late, I was never introduced as anything other than my parents' daughter. No self-righteous explanations about picking me out of the gutter or saving one of the less fortunate ever followed the introductions. My parents simply said, "This is our daughter Vicki."

Every year on the anniversary of when I came to live with them, my parents send me a card and tell me how lucky they are to have me in their life. Can you imagine, they saved my life and they are thankful? For our thirtieth "sister anniversary," I was surprised at work with a colorful bouquet of flowers from my sister Dawn, with a card that read, "I'm so glad you're my sister."

As adults, despite our intense Packer/Viking rivalry, Dawn and I are still kindred spirits and still little girls sharing secrets. I feel equally blessed by the support of my other adoptive sister, Gail. Without my asking, she and her husband Jan purchased my son's first set of leg braces to help me with his financial needs. Life circumstances made Dawn and Gail my sisters, but love made them my friends.

As a seven-year-old child, I was drowning in abandonment issues, loneliness, distrust, and fear. Even so, the moment I made eye contact with my adoptive parents, I knew deep inside that they were my rescuers and my family.

Today, I am thankful that they were not a temporary placement. That they chose to bring this heartbroken, "hard-to-place" little girl into their lives for the long haul. That they accepted me as a member of their family completely and unconditionally. Thirty-seven years later, my adoptive family still includes, supports, and loves me. I feel so blessed to have these angels in my life.

—Victoria Roder

Simply His Mother

I sat on the edge of my chair and clasped my hands in my lap to keep them from trembling. The air conditioner hummed and blew a cold breeze across my cheek, dissipating the stifling Vietnamese heat and humidity. My husband stood an arm's length away from me, video camera poised. How could he hold it so steady? A quiver of excitement ran through my body.

Pam, another woman on the same journey as us, sat on the couch next to me in the identical state of anticipation. She squeezed my hand. "Do you think they'll be here soon?"

I didn't trust my voice to answer her.

I couldn't stop staring at the doorway across the room from me. Moments before, an old, stooped lady disappeared around that corner to get our son. Our son.

He's not going to be the first one. He's not going to be the first one. I kept silently repeating that mantra so I wouldn't be disappointed when Pam's daughter was brought out before our son. I could wait a few more minutes.

My entire life had led up to this very moment— the moment I would become a mother for the first time. Years of negative pregnancy tests, intimate questions, invasive doctor's exams, hormones, elevator emotions, painful injections, surgeries, and failed fertility procedures had all led us to Hanoi on this oppressive July day. And in this place and time, our lives would change forever. Where once we had been a couple, just the two of us, now we would be a mommy and a daddy with a child, a family.

I heard voices and movement in the back room of the house. *Was he coming soon?* No one appeared at the door.

Doubts niggled the edge of my mind. In my heart, I already loved this child, even though I had only seen him in a few pictures. I had never held him or smelled his sweet baby scent. I'd never heard him cry or laugh. We had been told we wouldn't have to travel to Vietnam to complete the adoption of our son. He would be escorted to the United States, and we would meet him in an airport somewhere in the Midwest. But as we waited for the call that would let us know he was on his way home, the Vietnamese authorities had changed their policy and required parents to fly across the vast Pacific Ocean to register the adoption in person in country.

Our social worker informed us that we could transfer to another country without penalty if we didn't want to travel. I hate to fly, but how could I let go of the child whose big dark eyes had won my heart? I couldn't bear the thought of him becoming some other woman's son. He was mine.

Six weeks later, I sat waiting to meet him, fretting. *How would he feel about me? Would he arch his back or try to wriggle out of my grasp?* We had been warned that adopted children often did this at first in response to their new parents. *Would he cry or even scream when he saw me?* I shuddered at the thought of him being afraid of me. *After five months in an orphanage, would he be able to love me? Would I be able to love him as much as a child I might have nurtured in my own body?*

I snuck a glace at my husband. *Was he having the same doubts I was?* He'd been so strong and supportive in everything we'd been through the past few years. In fact, he was the first one to broach the subject of adoption. And his sense that we were doing the right thing had never wavered. But did he wonder if he could love this little boy who was about to become our son?

"Here he is."

I looked back to the corner of the room.

Did she say "he"? Is that my son in the doorway?

Before I could fully register what was happening, a young Vietnamese girl dressed in yellow handed me a baby. My baby. For the first time I felt the heat of his body through my cotton top. For the first time I felt the thumping of his heart against mine.

Sobs welled in my throat and my tears overflowed. I swallowed hard to stop them. I didn't want to frighten my son. I didn't want his first thoughts of me to be ones of fear.

Holding him away from me, I took my first good look at him. If you can call a boy beautiful, he was. He had a downy tuft of black hair on the top of his head, and I ran my hand over it. He had stubbly hair on the sides of his head, like it had been shaved within the past few days. He looked straight into my eyes, and I couldn't breathe. He knit his thick black eyebrows together, just like he had on one of the pictures sent to us months ago. We already called that his thinking expression and laughed about how he would keep us on our toes in the coming years.

My husband clicked off the camcorder and came to us.

"Here's your son." I passed our baby to him.

He dwarfed the tiny child who sat on his lap looking up at the man he would someday call Daddy. "Hello there. I'm your father," he murmured softly, as he smoothed the baby's black hair and kissed his forehead. "I love you." Overwhelmed, I'm sure, by all of the goings on, our son didn't smile, but he did study his father's face. Again, he crinkled his forehead, trying to understand what was happening to him.

I didn't think such joy existed as the joy that filled me while I watched the two men I loved most in the world get to know each other. I leaned against my husband's shoulder and stroked my son's back. Someone snapped a picture of the three of us, and in that instant as the bulb flashed, something almost indefinable happened. We became a family.

The questions that had raced through my mind mere minutes before now all had answers. A brief encounter with my new son was all I'd needed to know that what I felt for him was truly a mother's love. There was not a trace of doubt in my mind that I would play with him, teach him, feed him, cry for him, cheer for him, be there for him, and love him the way any mother would. My love was not determined by the shape of my son's eyes, the curve of his nose, the hue of his skin, or the blood in his veins. In fact, nothing he was or did influenced my feelings for him. He was simply my son. Nothing more and nothing less. And I was simply his mother. A mother who loved her son.

—*Liz Tolsma*

The Good, the Tough, and the Mommy

Adoption is like that proverbial box of chocolates: You never know what you're going to get.

As an attorney who handles adoption cases, I've found they run the gamut. For some, the sweetest moments of the parents' lives as they welcome a new life into their family; for others, despair as a birth mother changes her mind and keeps the baby at the last minute. International adoptions are a different animal, as parents spend outlandish amounts of money and two to five years waiting for a foreign child to arrive. Sometimes parents adopting foster children discover difficulties they never knew existed when the child was younger. What I never expected was that adoption would become a part of my own personal history.

I met my husband Eric through an online science fiction RPG group; our mutual interest in *Star Trek* led to the discovery of more common ground. We were both single parents; I had a nine-year-old daughter, and he had two sons, four years and eighteen months, and a four-month-old baby girl. I fell in love with his children, as I did with him, and we all became a family.

As I came to know the children better, I noticed little oddities. Mike, the oldest, talked "at" people, not "with" them. His precocious conversation didn't mesh with what went on around him. He didn't make eye contact. Middle child Will didn't talk. Most of his wants were requested by a high-pitched "Eeee! Eeeee!" Baby Tasha fixated on the ceiling fan for hours, watching it turn, and as she grew, she spent hours spinning and swinging. She didn't talk or make eye contact, either.

At first, Eric assured me that "boys were just different." What did I know? I'd raised five girls. They had engaged with others and conversed and joked— not like these boys, who couldn't remember what they were told for thirty seconds. Discipline didn't work. They'd often stare into space. They'd line up toys and eat inedible objects. *Is this really what boys do?* I wondered. *Can they be so different from girls?*

When Mike went to preschool, the teachers informed us his behavior was impossible to control. He would blurt out in class, and he was focused solely on his own wants and desires. We tried to work with him, but there was a breakdown in communication.

He didn't seem to speak the same language we did. He didn't take in what we said.

Will, by three years old, still didn't talk. At that point, I drew the line and requested services through early intervention. They had Eric sign the papers; I was only the stepmother. Though their birth mother left for the West Coast when the baby was four months old and never returned, the medical caregivers told me that, because of privacy rules, they could only deal with the biological father and mother. So sorry, they said.

In the next year, Tasha, too, started with early intervention, but her issues were more serious than just lack of speech. She seemed to be in another world, an internal world we couldn't reach. I read anything I could find, trying to figure out what might be going on. I tried to talk to the doctors but always got the same polite response: "You're not the mother."

Spending twenty-four hours a day, seven days a week with these children who plainly needed help, knowing professionals needed to be pushed to take action, and with my husband too busy and too inexperienced to deal with the multitude of issues, my frustration level hit the roof over the next twelve months. Four little letters: s-t-e-p. They didn't seem so big. But they made a world of difference in what I could do for these children.

We soldiered on. As Mike hit public school, the teachers and counselors found something definitely "wrong" with him. Though we'd been through evaluations, we hadn't been able to get anyone to diagnose him. The professionals always tested him in fifteen-minute sessions, one on one. But for fifteen minutes, with full attention on him, Mike shines. Sadly, life doesn't work that way. The school thought he should be able to cope in a class of twenty-three students for six hours, follow the rules, pay attention, and not believe the class revolved solely around him. With the school's file as fodder, we tried again with a pediatric neurologist, who took all of five minutes to tell us there was no question: the boy had Asperger's syndrome, an autism-spectrum disorder.

Tasha also went with us that day, and the doctor tried to be kind as he informed us she was autistic, as well, but with a much less hopeful future. "Static encephalopathy," he wrote on the sheet he gave us. I looked that up when we got home. It means "permanent or unchanging brain damage." It made me cry.

I grieved every bit as much as if these had been children of my womb. Autism is a stunning diagnosis; receiving two verdicts in the same day was very hard. On the other hand, knowing the reason for Mike's defiant and difficult behaviors actually made it easier to cope. Putting a name to these afflictions opened the door to help by way of interventions and wraparound services and therapy of many flavors. But there was one item to take care of first. I had to make these children mine if I was going to be able to help save them.

Once I'd drawn up adoption papers, we tracked down the mother through mutual friends. Though she'd abdicated her role years before, we had both tacitly understood that I would care for the children without asking for this sacrifice. So, of course, she was reluctant to give up her rights. When I explained the tragic extent of the situation and the reason I needed her to do this, she agreed at last, and with the best interests of the children at heart, she signed the consent forms. It was a true act of love for which I will always be grateful.

The actual adoption proceeding was nerve-wracking for me. I'd done dozens of them from the other side of the table. Now I was the one receiving the questions, and my husband was being asked to confirm his consent and to verify that I would be a good mother for his children, whose futures were hanging in the balance.

The court had called in a judge from out of town to make sure there was no appearance of favoritism by the county judges before whom I practiced all the time. He came right down off the bench and had a seat at the table with us, which really threw me off, as the judges I'd worked with had never done that. I stammered through my answers, gaining some valuable insight on what my clients went through, even on a happy occasion like an adoption hearing. Finally, the judge signed the three decrees. Congratulations, it's a boy! And a boy! And a girl! You can pass out the cigars now. Finally, I was able to act freely, attend appointments, and receive information.

Researching local facilities, we found and set up weekly speech therapy and occupational therapy sessions. Tasha began to overcome her sensory integration issues, which had made it agony even to comb her hair or to shop at Wal-Mart. The occupational therapist despaired whether Tasha would ever learn to use scissors. (Now she trims her own hair when no one's looking. Who knew?) We found an agency to teach social skills, which are usually lacking in children with autism, and we plunged right into remedial therapies that took as much as seventy hours a week among the three children.

Four years of wraparound services and mobile therapy combined with a school system justifiably proud of its autism support program has taken Mike through elementary school and into junior high. He loves singing in the chorus and has a fascination for comics. He's still very different from his classmates, but his intelligence comes through to allow him to make a good impression on his teachers.

Will was finally diagnosed with ADD, like his father, and a small dose of medication gets him back on track each morning. His teachers say he always knows the answers in class. He loves girls. Loves them. I can't wait for high school (not!). We're still working on his need to eat odd things, but hope that, too, will pass.

Tasha has made major progress with her language delays and is in age-appropriate fourth grade, spending half the day in a regular class and attending an autistic-support class for reading and math. She loves science and participates in 4-H activities. She laughs often, which she never did as a small child, and she squabbles with her brothers just like normal siblings. She has developed empathy and looks out for us as we look out for her.

Though I knew the children had issues when I adopted them, there are still surprises every day, some good, some not so good. By making this little family official, we have created a stable environment and a home full of love that will give these children the best possible chance to overcome their disabilities. Permanent brain damage? Not on my watch. Because I'm the mommy now.

—*Barbara Mountjoy*

As American as They Come

"If you were to get one of these dolls for your birthday, which one would you want?"

My soon-to-be eight-year-old daughter Alyssa belly-flopped onto the twin bed next to me, tucked her long, silky black hair behind her ear, and flipped open the catalog that had come in the mail that day.

"Let's see." She scanned the pages, past the 1940s doll and the Civil War doll, past the Native American and Hispanic ones. She paused for just a moment to examine the Revolutionary War doll more closely.

"Hmmm." She snapped back to the front. "This one."

I looked at the picture of the doll under her finger. A blonde-haired, blue-eyed girl dressed in bell-bottom jeans stared back at me.

"Are you sure?"

My daughter nodded, her teardrop-shaped eyes intent on the image in front of her. "That's the one I want."

I slid the catalog in front of me and turned a few pages until I saw the title, "A Friend that Looks Like You."

"You don't want one of these dolls?" I glanced at the one with the dark hair and dark eyes like my Korean-born child. Wouldn't she be happier with a doll that had the same Asian features as she did?

"No. I want the other one." I could tell by the adamant tone in her voice that Alyssa had made up her mind and I wouldn't be able to change it. I hoped she wouldn't be disappointed in her choice later on.

A few weeks later, my delighted birthday girl tore open the wrapping paper on her gift and discovered the box containing her new doll—blonde-haired and blue-eyed, just as ordered. As soon as she had the doll out of the packaging, she hugged it to her.

"Thanks Mom and Dad. I love her. She's the one I really, really wanted. Thank you, thank you."

Yes. Alyssa is as American as they come. No matter that her foster mother rocked her to sleep with Korean lullabies for the first three months of her life. No matter that her given name tastes strange on American tongues. No matter that, as I breathed in the first scent of my infant daughter, I was greeted not by a whiff of baby powder but by the smell of kim chee.

If you ask her to name her favorite food, she won't hesitate before answering, "Chicken McNuggets." When she tries to greet someone in Korean, her tongue ties in knots around the foreign words. She loves to lie on a blanket and watch the Fourth of July fireworks shooting off overhead and to run around the yard, the sparkler in her hand shooting stars into the grass.

Still, when we heard about a local group whose aim is to teach Korean culture to adoptees, she begged to join, and I obliged. The days ticked by for her until their next event, a Korean New Year celebration, rolled around. Eagerly, we set off that morning to celebrate the holiday with other children born in Korea but raised in America.

Similarly dark-skinned children and fair-skinned parents crowded the lobby of the church while flashes from digital cameras lighted the interior. "Mom, Mom, take a picture of me in my hanbok." Alyssa gave me a broad smile as she posed in the traditional green and red, high-waisted dress trimmed in gold someone had lent us.

The day began in the auditorium with a program of various Korean performing arts. Alyssa leaned forward in her seat, mouth agape as a dozen women swirled around the stage in shimmering white and gold hanboks. Her eyes widened when these same women performed the colorful fan dance. But she grew bored when a man in a stovepipe hat sang a ballad in Korean. "I can't understand him, Mom," she whispered to me.

So we set off in search of adventure. Several classrooms offered crafts for the children. First, Alyssa made a traditional Korean purse out of blue silk, and then she assembled a bright blue, yellow, and red fan.

Time flew by, and before we knew it, the ladies who had organized the event began serving lunch. We piled our plates high with bulgogi—a grilled beef dish marinated in soy sauce and sesame oil—sticky rice, Korean noodles, and Korean pancakes similar to egg foo young. While I got brave enough to put a small amount of kim chee on my plate, my daughter refused to touch the very spicy pickled cabbage with a ten-foot pole. She chatted all through the meal with another little girl her age with the same round face and smushed-in nose.

After devouring a couple of yummy Korean cookies, we set off again. This time we learned Korean paper-folding before heading over to the calligraphy room. Again, Alyssa's mouth hung open as the young

Korean woman painted her birth name on a sheet of parchment.

She clutched the paper to her chest as we left the area. "Can we hang this on the wall in my room when we get home?" I noticed her peek at it more than once during the remainder of the day.

We made our way to the next very American activity—face painting. Alyssa poured over the sheet of possibilities, her forehead creased in concentration. "I'll have this one," she decided at last. She sat perfectly still as the artist applied her chosen design to her face. She skipped out of the room, excited to show her new friends her art: I ♥ Korea.

Much too soon for Alyssa's taste, we began the journey home, with a stop at a local mall on the way to pick up a birthday gift for her brother. Her shoulders sagged as we rode the down escalator.

"Mom, will people think I'm weird with this on my face?" She caressed her cheek, displaying her heritage for the world to see.

What words could I offer to reassure her? I had to think on my feet. "Not at all. You're Korean as well as American. That's nothing to be ashamed of, nothing to hide. I think it's wonderful. And not many people are as lucky as you to be both."

She stood a little taller and held her head high as we fought the crowds through the stores. I noticed her touch her face from time to time.

Sure, my daughter is as American as they come. But she is also Korean, and she is learning the fine art of straddling two cultures, becoming proud of where she came from and who she is. This day was an important step in that process.

As I leaned over her bed that night and kissed her on the forehead, she reached up and wrapped me in a bear hug. "Thank you, Mom. Today was the best day of my life."

—Liz Tolsma

The Real Deal

"Then Jonathon and Angie are your half brother and half sister," my friend Belinda announced to me.

As part of a school project we had been working on our family trees. Belinda had just finished looking at mine.

"They are not," I said. I slumped into my chair and tipped my head forward, my hair tumbling around my face.

"Yes, they are," she told me. "They'd only be your full brother and sister if you shared the same father and mother."

This was news to me. I shook my head in disbelief. We'd never used the terms *half brother* or *half sister* in our house. I was twelve years old, and it had never occurred to me that I was any different from my siblings. Now, here it was in black and

white in front of me: Jonathon and Angie were my
half brother and half sister. I found this distressing,
because it made me feel as though I didn't fit in with
my own family.

Later that night I discussed the issue with my
mother.

"Darling, Jonathon and Angie are as much your
brother and sister as they are to each other," she told
me. "Your father adopted you because he chose to be
your father. He wanted to be your parent in every
way possible, including taking on his name."

"What about Wayne?" I asked.

"It's not that he didn't want you," she said. "He
was incapable of being a father. In the beginning,
he did say he'd fight for custody of you. By the time
we went to court, he never showed up for the hearing. He did this on two occasions before the judge
decided to permit the adoption. Perhaps Wayne
understood what was best for you."

My mother and biological father, Wayne, had
separated when I was eight months old. Of course, I
was too little to have any memories from this time.
By the time I was eighteen months old, my mother
had met and fallen in love with Dave, the man who
legally became my father when I was three years old.
At the time, my parents had recently married and
were expecting my baby brother.

Dave is the only father I've ever known. I can count on two hands the number of times I've met with Wayne. Yet, I can't remember ever being sat down and told I was adopted. I just always knew. Apparently, in the beginning, I called Dave "Daddy Dave," and on the odd occasion I saw Wayne, he was "Daddy Wayne." Then, without encouragement from my parents, I dropped "Daddy" from "Wayne" and began referring to Dave as simply "Daddy." I guess even as a toddler I knew what felt right.

Over the years, people who don't know me well have said I look like my adopted dad. Apparently, we have the same dark eyes and dark hair. I've never corrected them. Secretly, I liked the comparison. It made me feel like I actually was his biological daughter.

Growing up, I rarely gave Wayne much thought. As a small child, there were infrequent visits on birthdays and Christmas, but after I turned ten, all contact ceased. I liked it that way, because it meant I didn't have to think about being adopted. As far as I was concerned, Dave was my father. Wayne was a stranger to me, and I had no desire to develop a relationship with him.

When I was well into my teenage years, I received a phone call from Wayne. He was living in another state and had returned to South Australia for a holiday. He told me he'd like to see me again. I agreed, mostly out of curiosity. It had been eight years since I'd last seen or heard from him.

When he stood in front of me, I gave him a stiff hug. There was no connection between us. I searched his face for any resemblance of myself but found nothing. That meeting with Wayne ended up being awkward and short. We made some small talk, and soon after I made my excuses to leave.

As I walked up the driveway afterward, I made a decision: I was never going to pursue a relationship with him. I wasn't angry, sad, or bitter. It's just that I realized in that moment that I had a father already. There was no void in my life to fill. Dave had been there for me since I was a baby. He'd nursed me through the measles, sat through countless dance recitals, and provided a roof over my head and a safe, loving environment to grow up in. Wayne had missed everything, and there was no going back.

I didn't struggle with this decision nor shed any tears. I got the feeling that Wayne no more wanted a relationship with me than I did him. He seemed content with his life, and I was more than happy with mine.

In the years that followed, I never gave Wayne a second thought. I actually had to remind myself that I was adopted. There were times when I wondered how my adopted father's family viewed me. Did his parents consider me to be one of their "real" grandchildren? Was my name included in the family Bible I've heard mentioned? I don't know the answers to these questions because I've never seen the Bible and I've never discussed my feelings with my grandparents. I guess these things were important to me in the past because I wanted to feel accepted—but not because my parents ever treated me differently from my siblings.

We are a close family, and we've never spoken of me being a half sister to either Jonathon or Angie. That's why I was surprised when my mother suggested that I ask my father to walk me down the aisle.

"Why do you want me to do that?" I asked.

"I think he's worried that you might want Wayne to do it," my mum said.

I raised my eyebrows. I didn't think of Wayne as my father. Why would I want him to give me away?

Sensing my surprise, my mum said to me, "Your father didn't want to take it for granted that he would be giving you away. I know it's been on his mind, and if you don't ask him, he's not going to know how you feel."

I couldn't believe that for one minute he'd think I'd want anyone other than him to give me away.

"Mum," I said, "I'm not even inviting Wayne to the wedding. He's had nothing to do with me my whole life. Why on earth would I even consider asking him to give my hand away in marriage?"

"You need to tell your father that," she told me.

I did ask Dad to walk me down the aisle. When the day arrived, my mother told me she'd never seen him look so proud. As we walked down the aisle, arm in arm, I saw the emotion in his face. He'd never been one for crying, but I could see he was choked up. He was holding his upper lip stiffly, and his eyes appeared slightly misty. It was a touching moment for the two of us, one I'll never forget.

I feel lucky that my step-father chose to accept me as his daughter. Now that I'm a grown woman with three daughters of my own, I know that they are lucky to have him as a grandfather, too. In all the ways that count, he is my real dad, and in every way, we are a real family.

—Lindee Nearmy

Invisible Bonds

When my adopted son, Sam, was two years old, he suddenly began acting out a fantasy several times each day. He was a firefighter who was desperately and unsuccessfully trying to save someone on the second floor of a building. He would always fall back down to the floor below and with renewed determination repeat his frantic ascent to the second floor. At no time in his short life had he ever witnessed a fire or known anyone who had suffered from a fire. No amount of cajoling, comforting, or acting it out with him brought Sam any relief.

After several weeks, his need to indulge this fantasy waned. I was left with a strong impression that he was connecting with someone who was important to him. It was several years before I discovered it was his birth father, whom we had never met.

Our adoption of Sam began with a phone call from his birth mother, Julie. Within minutes, she and I felt a powerful, mysterious bond that carried us through the intense feelings of elation and sadness, of completion and loss, of devotion and love for this beautiful boy born just thirty-six hours later. Knowing that my husband and I would be unable to catch a flight in time for his unexpectedly early birth, Julie offered phone contact throughout her labor. By the time Sam was born, I felt a destined bond resembling the intensity and headiness of falling in love—a bond not only with this baby but also with his courageous, determined mother. I realized that my desire to mother Sam was just as strong as my vow to cherish Julie and to honor his birth family with as much contact as I could create. It was many years before I was able to fulfill this vow completely.

Postplacement, I was struck by my strong yearning for contact with Julie. At that time, I took an unscientific survey of other adoptive mothers and discovered that their feelings mirrored mine. Even those who had made closed adoption plans had daily thoughts of the birth mother's health and well-being.

Contact with Julie helped me stay grounded in my role in Sam's life and thereby helped me to be a better parent. In our openness, Julie and I bestowed upon each other a precious entitlement for the very different ways in which we each were his mother. Our clarity about our roles and our ability to keep Sam's best interest as the focus felt deeply satisfying to me.

Within a few months, however, Julie chose not to maintain openness with us. Meeting Sam's birth father, Paul, was even farther on the horizon. I prayed every day that somehow, someday, all our families would connect.

During the subsequent years, Sam developed his musical talent, inherited from Julie and wholeheartedly supported by me. I fulfilled my promise to her to make sure he learned to swim.

When Sam was four, we adopted another boy, Matt. With his birth mother, Claire, I also developed a deep connection, from our first phone call two months before his birth through coaching her in the delivery room, through the day she and Matt were discharged from the hospital. On that momentous day, my feelings were swinging from ecstasy at the thought of mothering this beautiful baby boy to acute pain as I witnessed Claire's stoic grief.

As we were leaving the hospital, Claire and I experienced a spiritual moment so profound that it was two weeks before we could even speak of it. With Matt in my arms, I walked next to Claire down the entry hall. When we were about twenty feet from the main doors, it was as if time stopped. Suddenly, I could no longer hear or see any of the people walking by us, except for a tall, slim woman of indeterminate age. Dressed in white, she approached Claire with an air of boundless love. We stopped. The woman placed her hand on Claire's right shoulder and asked, "Are you okay?" It didn't sound to me like a question, but rather like a blessing of love and acceptance that she was beaming into Claire. There was a visible shift in Claire, and I knew that she had received the woman's powerful gift. She passed between us, and I could again hear and see people around us. Quickly, I looked behind us to catch one more look at this miraculous woman, but she had literally vanished. We moved toward the large double doors, this time with a kind of glow around Claire, who had more confidence in her step.

From time to time, Claire and I recall her guardian angel, and we marvel at her timely appearance, apparently visible only to the two of us.

When Sam was nine years old, his questions about his birth and my interest in knowing how Julie was faring became more persistent. With some fear that I might find a closed door, I searched for her. When we made contact, I found a young woman who had matured considerably and was ready to renew openness with us.

The day Julie drove to our home to see Sam for the first time since his birth, we waited anxiously for her car to appear in the driveway. Even though I had sent her pictures of the boys, I knew that seeing them in person would be a whole different experience for her. I was also aware of my own desire for her genuine approval of how I was raising Sam and Matt.

We rushed out of the house when she pulled up, and I enveloped her in a huge hug that felt like welcoming home a long-lost daughter. Julie welcomed all questions from Sam about his beginnings and about her choice to place him for adoption. One of the most memorable moments of that visit for me was when Julie and Sam created music together. When I heard Julie's beautiful voice accompanied by Sam's drumming, the love that can come full circle in open adoption was palpable.

The ease with which we maneuvered that first reunion weekend paved the way for all our future visits. For Julie, reopening the adoption entailed facing the implications of keeping Sam's birth a secret from everyone in her life, both family and friends.

Over the course of the next few years, Julie's forgiveness of herself helped to release her from self-blame and shame. When she was able to share with her loved ones the news of Sam's birth and her choice to place him for adoption, it healed a deep wound in her and enabled her to develop a closer relationship with her family.

In one of my conversations with Julie, I asked if she had ever experienced a fire. I learned that at the very time two-year-old Sam was acting out his fire scene, she and his birth father had driven home to find their second floor apartment on fire. Unaware that a neighbor had been able to save their dogs, Paul had frantically attempted to reach their apartment. The smoke had forced him to retreat back down the stairs.

I renewed my effort to reach out to more of Sam's birth family and continued to extend an invitation to Paul. Children have a way of inspiring us to look within ourselves and to grow, and that's what Paul's second son, Joe, did for him. When Joe was two and Sam was fifteen, I received a call from Paul. He was ready to see Sam and ready to tell his family the long-kept secret of his first son. It was an extremely emotional, healing time for Paul, and within a few weeks, I traveled with Sam and Matt to spend a few days with Sam's extended paternal birth family.

Before that ten-hour car trip, I had spoken extensively with Paul and with his parents, Steven and

Jane. Overriding all their emotions was an intention to do what was best for both Sam and Matt. Jane has always asked, "Is this best for the boys? We want our presence in their lives to be positive."

For me, seeing Sam with his birth father, birth grandparents, great-grandmother, aunts, uncles, and cousins felt like a necessary gift for his maturing identity. Every night of that first visit was a celebration dinner. They said they were keeping the number at twenty in order not to overwhelm Sam. They promised that the next time, they would invite the whole family and rent a hall big enough for 150 people. By the time we departed for home, Jane had hung a picture of Sam and Matt on her wall of grandchildren photos.

Since that visit, we have seen Sam's birth family on both sides numerous times. We cherish the memories of Claire's wedding, the birth of Matt's half brother, Julie's wedding, and the birth of Sam's half sister. My sons are now twelve and seventeen, and I still feel fathomless appreciation for these two young women who were brave enough to have these incredible children and trusted me enough to be their mother. My appreciation also comes from their generosity in sharing their families and subsequent children, so that my sons can know all their siblings. It also comes from the privilege of witnessing and nourishing those bonds that inherently exist among members of adoptive and birth families.

I expect that, in years to come, we will meet other birth family members. An ever-reaching tree, our roots and branches multiply and grow stronger.

When Sam was six years old, he did an exercise with me. We traced his hands on a large piece of paper. One hand he designated as his adoptive family, the other as his birth family. He filled each hand with interests, achievements, and talents that he attributed to each family. There were a couple of things he said didn't belong to either family, so we made a "Just Sam" list below the hands. My heart filled with awe when he drew a line connecting the hands and the "Just Sam" list and said, "These are all connected, and you have to keep going back and forth, back and forth."

—*Debra Feintech*

The Journey to Me

Adoption does not begin nor end when loving parents "choose a child." Indeed, adoption is a lifelong journey filled with ups and downs, joys and sorrows, experiences and emotions that are unique to each person. I am a chosen child, and I am living that very personal journey.

I was around five years old when I was officially told that I was adopted. Almost thirty years later, I remember it as clearly as if it were yesterday.

It started with my brother, five years older than me. Frustrated with something that I, his pain-in-the-neck little sister, had done, he came to me with anger sparking in his brown eyes.

"You're adopted," he spat.

He towered over me, his face flush with the pride of being older, smarter, bigger, and in possession of ominous knowledge. I knew instinctively that, in his mind, being adopted was undesirable and a way of being able to hurt my feelings. But to my utter frustration, I didn't really know what it meant.

All of that frustration churned inside, and I rose up, my hands firmly planted on my hips, and proclaimed, "No, I am not!"

He laughed, his eyes twinkling with mischief and sneered, "You don't even know what it means."

"Yes, I do!" I retorted, my little face screwing up with aggravation at having to lie to cover my ignorance. Welling up with angry tears, I stormed off to play with my dolls.

As time generally escapes a child, I have no idea how long I had been playing before I ran to the living room to fetch something I had left there. Our living room was large and separated from the kitchen and dining room by wooden railings. It was early afternoon, the light beaming through the large picture window, but it seemed the easy chair, where my mom sat, was in shadows. Even to my young, inexperienced eyes, it appeared that she was lost in thought, her mind occupied. Intuitively, I approached her with caution.

"Susan, I have something I need to tell you," she paused, exhaling deeply and inhaling slowly before continuing, "Something I should have told you a long time ago."

The way she said those words made my heart skip a beat, and I turned to look at her, my mind racing, trying to think of all of the things I could possibly be in trouble for. Then she stood and invited me to go for a walk with her. That walk changed my world and how I fit into it.

We lived on a mixed farm on the Alberta prairies, a beautiful place nestled in a small valley that my father had taken over from his father. Mom chose to walk down the "east road," as we called it, a dirt road built mainly for machinery to access the fields east of the farm. It must have been early spring, because I remember having to wear a coat to shut out the chill. I walked beside Mom with a stomach full of butterflies, stealing quick glances at her face as I tried to figure out what she needed to say to me.

I cannot remember the exact words that transpired, but I remember well the sentiment of the experience and my feelings at the time. After walking in silence for some distance, my mom finally turned to me and told me that she loved me.

"I love you too, Mommy," I happily replied, relieved that, whatever was to come, it wasn't due to my having done something bad.

She then explained to me that mommies and daddies all over the world are happy when they get to have children, but that some mommies and daddies are not able to have children at all. Happy not to be in trouble, I eagerly listened to her words but wondered why she was telling me this, because my mommy and daddy had two children.

Mom went on to explain that some mommies aren't able to look after their children, so they give them to people who really want to have babies but can't. She told me that I was one of those babies and that they were the mommy and daddy who could not have kids. This was called "adoption."

Confused, I stopped walking. My mind had been picturing a lovely scene in which a young woman tenderly and lovingly handed over a baby (dressed in the frilly pink dress that my rub-a-dub dolly wore) to another woman, and they are all smiles and so proud. But when my mom uttered that word— *adoption*—visions of my brother and his use of the word as an insult cut through my daydream like a sword, slicing it to ribbons and scattering it in the wind. My mom had made it sound happy, but my brother had made it sound bad. Which was it?

If only I'd had the insight and emotional intellect to express those thoughts then; I wonder how different my life would have been. Perhaps the confusion and dichotomy of my life could have been resolved in that instant. Much later, as an adult, I read somewhere about the "primordial pain of adoption"—the pain of newborns being taken away from their birth mothers at such an important bonding time in their lives. Looking back, I know that I felt a deep pain when I was told about being adopted, and I eventually came to understand this pain as loss and sadness. It was almost as if being told I was adopted had resurrected the grief and the longing for the connection I'd had with the woman who had carried and given birth to me.

I cried, and my mom hugged me and cried in my hair. I hugged her back as great sobs shook my body. She continued to tell me that they loved me like I was their own child, like my brother was. The sneer and the degrading way he'd said adopted suddenly then made sense to me. I was different from him. He was theirs. This sudden realization shocked me, and the tears stopped briefly. "How come you just didn't make more babies?" I inquired quietly.

My mom explained that they tried to have another baby for a long time. When they discovered they could not, they decided to adopt a baby instead.

Having always been the inquisitive sort, I questioned her on the whole adoption process, and as she spoke, the grief I had been experiencing slowly dissipated. Mom reminisced about waiting for a match, finally being told they could get me, and the joy they'd felt in adopting and raising me. My heart felt lighter, and my smile widened as she described how they felt when they first saw me. They had to drive to Edmonton to get me, and on the way home they'd stopped to surprise Grandma and Grandpa, who didn't know I was coming. My mind envisioned a happy picture of my mommy and daddy lovingly picking me up (in the frilly pink dress that my rub-a-dub dolly wore) and presenting me to my new family.

Happily, I grabbed my mom's hand and skipped home, letting the happy scene replay itself over and over in my mind. The grief and loss were forgotten for the time being. The next time my brother sneered at me that I was adopted, I happily agreed. I felt special, being with the mommy and daddy who had wanted me so much.

As I matured, the feelings of grief and loss reoccurred, and I didn't understand them. Deep feelings emanating from my core and an unexplained longing would overtake me unexpectedly. I kept it mostly to myself. I didn't understand the emotions I was experiencing, much less articulate them to anyone else. I'm sure I sometimes appeared moody to those around me. Those feelings grew along with my body, until, as a young adult, I finally recognized them for what they were. And then I desperately longed to know more about what made me *me*.

Over time, the differences between my adoptive family and I became more evident. Conversely, the similarities between my brother and our parents also became more evident. At each developmental stage, I gained a new and different perspective on adoption itself, and with my newfound perspectives, I would measure who I was and how I fit into my world. Being the inquisitive person I have always been, I wanted to know more. I longed to be like someone, to look like someone, to sound like someone, to be "a chip off the old block."

Through postadoption support services, I was able to locate and meet various members of my birth family. It was a scary undertaking. I was terrified that I would hurt my parents' feelings or offend them by doing so. I was uncertain about what I would learn about my genetic history and about my birth family. A niggling fear of being rejected by them developed in my heart. I didn't know if I had the strength to be rejected by them a second time.

Finally, I found the courage to tell my parents that I had found out more information about my birth family. I think that shocked them a bit, but the words that my father spoke took my breath away.

"Susan, we always knew this could happen, right from the day we got you. If you need any help, we are here." He hugged me close then, and in that instant,

I knew I had been loved unconditionally. Despite my grief and longing, despite my differences, uncertainties, and insecurities, my parents had loved me as one of their own. Again, I cried. Again, I felt special.

As I move through my life, the "primordial wound" is healing. As I nurture who I am and remain open to the love of the many people around me, I see the wondrous part of me that is able to shine no matter what situation I am in. Finding my birth family has helped, although the love of my parents has been paramount. The birth of my children has also taught me much. And I am still learning.

One thing I have learned is that adoption is not the sum total of my life; rather, it is a vital part of my path to follow in this life. Being a special "chosen child" has helped to shape me and has helped me to discover who I am at the deepest levels. Adoption is a lifelong personal journey that has added an extra level to solving the riddle of me. I am thankful for all I have learned and experienced for all I continue to learn and experience along the way.

—*Susan R. Kostuch*

The Outlaws

Everyone had gathered in a sun-dappled back-yard in eastern Colorado on a beautiful September day to celebrate Ettie's 100th birthday. My husband and I joked that we felt like outlaws—one step removed from in-laws. We could tell that some of the guests were wondering who we were. We didn't look like the rest of the dark-haired, dark-eyed family. All Ettie's living children, grandchildren, great-grand-children, and great-great-grandchildren, along with various other relatives and friends, had come together to honor her. And we were there, too—the outlaws.

Our two adopted children, Jerry and Terry, are Ettie's grandchildren by birth. How we came to adopt them and then came to this family gathering more than thirty years later is a long story. It began when a doctor told us the chance of our having a baby was a million to one.

"So, if you're thinking about adopting, go ahead," he said bluntly, dismissing us to get on with patients he could actually help.

We talked to a social worker, who said the waiting period for a white infant was at least five years.

I looked up, surprised, "Oh, it doesn't have to be a white infant," I said. "We'd consider any child."

"Even siblings?" she asked. I could almost see her running through case files in her head.

"Sure," I said. "But not more than four. We only have three bedrooms."

My husband looked at me like I'd lost my mind but said nothing.

A few weeks later, we were looking at pictures of the cutest little seven-year-old boy and five-year-old girl imaginable. All we were told about their birth family was that their mother had died, their father had been given a year to make a home for them and hadn't, their grandmother was taking care of her ailing husband and couldn't physically or financially care for them, too, and they had several half-siblings who were teenagers. Open adoptions in which birth families and adoptive families were allowed to interact weren't even considered back then. We understood that we wouldn't be given any more information and that the birth family would be given no information about us.

Frankly, caught up in the excitement of finally becoming parents, we weren't very interested in the kids' past history. When the adoption was finalized, we were handed their new birth certificates to make sure all our names were spelled correctly. Their original certificates were attached by mistake. That's how we came to know their original last name and birth place. It was an unusual name and stuck in my memory even after I handed the certificates back to the clerk.

The road was not smooth. Because the two kids had been taken from a large extended family and placed in a series of foster homes before being declared adoptable, they had many problems. Most of the time, just surviving from day to day was all we could manage.

Just when it seemed we were making progress, they became teenagers and regressed, their emotional and behavioral problems multiplying. In addition, there were health issues. The doctor wanted a complete family medical history. We had always told the kids that when they were both eighteen we'd help them find their birth family, of whom they still had some vague memories. We decided not to wait. They needed answers right away, even though they were only thirteen and fifteen.

I knew my mother-in-law had a friend with the same last name as the kids, who also had come from the same county they did. I called and asked my husband's mother to see what she could find out. It was almost too easy. The woman remembered a relative whose two youngest children had been placed for adoption after her death. She gave us the phone number for one of the half-siblings of those children. I called the number.

Pat, the youngest of their five siblings, answered, and I said, "I think I'm the mother of your little brother and sister."

She said, "We have wanted to find you. We were going to search when the kids were older."

Many phone calls and a few weeks later, we had our first meeting with the family. By then, we were living ten hours away in western Colorado and we also had another child—that one in a million the doctor had told us about. She was ten years old, twelve years younger than her two siblings, and didn't understand all this adoption stuff. As far as she was concerned, all her relatives were theirs and all theirs should be hers, too. Fortunately, the birth family agreed and treated her just like they did Jerry and Terry.

We couldn't believe how much their Grandma Ettie, who was now a widow, was like Grandma

Campion, my husband's mother—similar in age, background, lifestyle, and interests. The family brought the kids each a box of mementoes of their early years—rubber toy animals, the vases from their mother's new baby bouquets, a few articles of clothing. And baby pictures! Terry, especially, had missed not knowing what she looked like as a baby. Once, when Terry was in grade school, her teacher had assigned the students to each bring a baby picture so everyone could guess who was who. Because the earliest picture we had of Terry was at five, everyone guessed her right away and she was so disappointed.

From that very first meeting, we all got along well and felt comfortable together. For the rest of their growing-up years, the kids made several individual trips to see their birth family. Terry came back from spending Thanksgiving with them with family recipes she insisted we try. Jerry was thrilled to have an older brother he looked and acted like, and Terry had a same-age cousin who could be her twin. Several members of the family came to Terry's college graduation. While the kids loved finding out about their relatives and ancestry, they always considered our house their home and us their parents. We never felt threatened or left out by their birth family.

That brings us back to the 100th birthday party. We had celebrated Grandma Campion's 98th birthday

Kissed by an Angel

The sweet cry of a newborn ended the young woman's long labor and my long wait for a daughter. After hours of intense but unproductive contractions, the doctor had determined that a Cesarean section was the safest option.

The adoption agreement allowed me to be present for the birth, and in the operating room I shook and held back tears while this brave woman—a girl, really—lay peacefully, accepting the situation, confident in her choice, while the obstetrician worked with precise skill. Finally, the doctor lifted the pink and squawking bundle into the world, and my heart caught in my throat as I gazed at the beautiful child who would be mine—a perfect baby, lovely in every way. Later, photographs would reveal that her grand entrance was a bit bloodier than I'd seen through my new mother's eyes.

My heart soared when the doctor announced the baby was a girl. I had two little boys at home, whom I loved dearly, but anyone who has a couple of little boys knows that they can be wild. Living on a farm had given them the chance to explore mud and slimy creatures on a regular schedule. No hike was complete to them if they hadn't carried a stick and whacked at every living plant and pine cone and rock along the way. I loved exploring the world through their eyes, but I'd longed to have a daughter to share the feminine side of life. The idea of soft pink sleepers alongside my laundry baskets of dirty denim gave me joy.

After our tiny newborn was given a thorough checkup and bundled tightly in a warm receiving blanket, I was told to take her to the nursery on the next floor. A kind nurse escorted me, which was a good thing, because, as excited as I felt, I may have gotten lost wandering about the huge building with my daughter in her rolling bassinette. I couldn't wait to introduce my little daughter to her father, and the elevator seemed to be moving slower than ever before.

Finally, the elevators opened, and there was my husband, sitting on a long bench in the hall, light streaming over him from the window behind. He stood, staring at me with questioning eyes. I knew what he wanted to know: was it a girl or a boy? My throat felt constricted with emotion. Taking a deep unsteady breath, I squeaked out "girl." We embraced and looked down into her sweet little face, at the delicate features and deep blue eyes, surrounded by wisps of dark-brown hair. Her head, misshapen from hours of labor, was encircled by a red ring that the doctor had called a halo.

The nurse ushered us into the nursery, where a new nurse took over but not before sharing in our excitement. I liked her immediately. After attaching matching wristbands to my husband, me, and our daughter, she painted each of the baby's feet with black ink and pressed the print onto paper records.

Then she unwrapped the tiny infant, checked her umbilical cord, and laid her on a warm towel. The baby stared with wide eyes at the new world, her mouth shaped into a perfect circle. With warm water, the nurse began to bathe her, pouring the water over her body and wiping her clean. A high-pitched cry escaped our daughter's now pinched little face. Her first bath wasn't to her liking. I wanted so much to pick her up and comfort her. The nurse turned her gently to the left, washing her right side. Then she turned her over on the other side. Suddenly, she hesitated, leaning down to take a closer look.

"Your baby has an unusual birthmark," she said, stopping to make a quick note in the chart.

Fear flooded me, and my heart raced. Was something wrong? I moved closer to get a good look and felt the tingle of amazement run down my arms.

My heart rate slowed back to its normal rhythm. I'd seen this mark before. After giving birth to our first child, the doctor had laid him on my chest with a blanket draped over his squirming body. Lifting the blanket to check every inch of him, my eyes caught sight of a round, red birthmark in the center of his chubby left hip. The doctor had examined it and declared it harmless.

Soon, we started calling the mark an "angel kiss." Our son, now five, would announce his special birthmark with pride, explaining that it was where an angel had kissed him before he was born. It was the same shape and at the same location as the precious mark on my new daughter.

"Our son has the same birthmark," I said.

The nurse looked up at me, questioning in her eyes. Next to me, my husband nodded his confirmation, and I felt his arm tighten around my waist. What an amazing gift. In that moment, I knew that this baby was meant for our family.

Today, our daughter is a lively eight-year-old. The opposite of her brothers, she loves to dance, ride horses, and plan her wedding. She now has a little sister only sixteen months younger. I couldn't be happier with my family. We have been blessed with four children, three through the miracle of adoption. Someone once told me that I would someday be thankful for not getting pregnant again, that I would be able to look back and see the blessings. I'm there right now.

Our children came to us in different ways. One was born to us, one came to us through an infant adoption, and two of them were toddlers when they came home. The one thing that was the same with each child was that the instant I first saw them, they became part of my heart. And in that blessed moment, I knew that I, too, had been kissed by an angel.

—*Christina S. Nelson*

His Gift and His Burden

Dereck is psychic.

That's the only way I can explain it.

I caught him at his computer long after his bedtime on Thursday night, picking at the keys. "Dereck, you're supposed to be in bed! What are you doing?"

"Nothing." He quickly turned off the screen and jumped into bed.

In the morning, when I woke him up for summer camp, I asked him again what he'd been doing.

"Writing a letter to my mom." He looked up at me, his lip quivering.

"Do you miss her?"

A nod and tears.

"Are you worried about her?"

Another nod, more emphatic, and more tears.

Of our three boys, Dereck is the most emotionally attached to his mother. He'd treated her like a doll, combing her hair and murmuring comfort to her when she was coming off a drug high and too catatonic to take care of them.

Since he's been with us, there are times when he suddenly gets very emotional and agitated about her, worried whether she is okay. Every time, we've discovered, it's connected to her effort to have contact with the boys. We'd find that, on a day when Dereck had a meltdown, she'd been calling the social worker a dozen times, screaming and pleading for contact, or she'd called the court, doing the same.

She continues to deny her drug problem, even though Dereck was born addicted to cocaine and crystal meth. During the supervised visitations she was allowed while the boys were in foster care, she had a habit of disappearing into the bathroom three and four times, coming out wiping her nose. After every drug test came back positive, the court finally gave up on her.

We'd opened a post office box for her so she could write to them. It took her more than a year to write, and the day the first letter landed in the mailbox, Dereck had had a meltdown before it arrived.

So, today, I knew something was up.

"Did you finish your letter?"

He told me no.

"Why don't you finish it before camp, and we'll mail it later?"

On the way to camp, he sat in the car next to me, miserable. He put his hand on my forearm and squeezed hard, and the tears flowed.

"Why don't we check the post office box today and see if your mom wrote?"

He nodded and worked hard to compose himself before he had to face his buddies at camp.

I read his letter after I came back. For the first time, he included his birth dad, who had been jailed for domestic violence. Their birth dad had walked away when the boys' mom had been arrested the last time, and the boys had been placed in foster care. He'd told the social worker, "This is too damned hard. You deal with it."

The boys had never seen him again, and the courts could never locate him. As far as we knew, their mom, who'd moved out of state, had no contact with him either.

But Dereck's letter was written as if they were together. I was puzzled.

After camp, we went to the box, and sure enough, there was a letter.

At the end, she'd written, "Your father called me and wanted to move here with me, but I have had too many heartaches with him, so I said no. I know your dad would be very proud of all of you. Would you like him to know how you are?"

Yep. Dereck is psychic.

He decided to change his letter a bit and added a postscript, telling his mom to let their dad know they were happy.

He finished the letter, and just like every time before, a burden was lifted from his shoulders. Whatever this thing was that got hold of him, the connection he still didn't understand, it had passed. He could get back to being a kid.

He and his brothers ran out to play catch in the yard, and I could hear him yelling and screaming with delight.

—John Sonego

Never Too Late

I loved being an adopted kid in the simpler years of the early thirties. It meant I was specially chosen from all the babies in the state children's home. As my parents' only child, I often asked why they didn't adopt a baby brother or sister for me. Mom always answered the same "We've thought about it often, dear. Wouldn't a little Jimmy be lots of fun?" she hinted. But after waiting on tenterhooks, my dreams of a sibling finally faded.

Holidays were awesome in our home, and photos capturing good times shared with family, young friends, and travels filled album after album. Only once in grade school can I recall being teased about being adopted, in response to which I proudly told my classmates that I'd been specially picked. And I had no burning desire to know who my biological parents were; it simply never mattered.

It was only after my mother followed my father in death that I discovered copies of my hospital birth papers amongst her belongings. I was mystified to learn that I had been named "Hannah Lee Batchelder." The documents revealed no other pertinent information. *Was this last name real or an alias for convenience?* I pondered. For the first time, in my late fifties, I experienced curiosity pangs and the need to find my biological parents. With the encouragement of my husband and my grown children, I began to search for my birth family. A kind soul gave me the name of an adoptees rights league, which resulted in lengthy forms. Because adoption records were closed in my birth state, I was assigned an intermediary.

"One or both of your biological parents could be living with family, in a rest home, or even deceased," warned the volunteer, an adoptee herself. Her story echoing mine, she cautioned me of pitfalls in searches for the elderly. "It is possible that you were born out of wedlock or abandoned in the wake of the country's hardships. The truth might be more than your biological parents would want revealed in their decline," she advised.

But with hope and unrelenting curiosity mounting, I pressed on with patience and determination as my daily guide. After four years of fruitless searching,

I was on the verge of giving up when my intermediary phoned unexpectedly on a hot July afternoon.

"Hi, Kathe. Are you sitting down? I've just come from a delightful visit with your birth mother in her apartment." Her verve zipped through the phone lines like a welcome breeze.

I paced back and forth, pressing the receiver tight against my ear, devouring every word as she described the woman who gave me life. Wilma Batchelder Chalmers was a perky, divorced, seventy-six-year-old redhead who was still running her floral business while recovering from a stroke. So that's where my red hair came from! Pictures and phone numbers were exchanged, but the intermediary said that Wilma needed time to contemplate a reunion.

Because I had instigated the search, I felt it was my place to contact Wilma first. For several days, I thought about calling her, but the time never seemed quite right. A few days passed, and then, while home alone one evening, I simply took my heart in my hands, picked up the phone, called and introduced myself. Wilma apologized for her slightly impaired speech, but she was the most upfront and gregarious stranger I had ever visited with. We discovered more about each other as people, about our families, and about our joys and sorrows than could possibly be absorbed in one sitting.

Wilma had been placed in a home for unwed mothers, far from her family, on the pretext of an extended holiday. An elderly maiden aunt had offered to make arrangements for Wilma's care, my birth, and eventual adoption. After all, society didn't look favorably upon young ladies caught in this condition in the 1930s, and utmost secrecy seemed crucial for her affluent family.

"I held you just once," Wilma's words faltered in a rush of tears. "Signing you away was the toughest day of my life, and I've thought about you every day, my dearest girl."

My insides quivered as her sweet voice spilled her inner-most secrets. "I have a lovely son and beautiful grown granddaughters," her words rang proud. "My son must never know about you, and I won't talk about your father, who is long dead and gone."

I promised to keep her secret, and my family and I made plans to visit her in the fall.

In the weeks that followed, I often wondered whether Wilma would remember my sixty-third birthday, and I tried hard to brush off the thought, knowing of her struggles in rebounding from a stroke. Then one day an envelope with Wilma's name and address handwritten in the corner arrived in the mail. Tears of joy slid off my chin as I sat in my pickup at our rural mailbox, ripping open the yellow envelope like an excited child. Wilma's high school graduation picture fell into my lap, a virtual mirror image of my own. A barely legible note inside the birthday card read: "*My Dearest Hannah Lee, Have a lovely day. Wilma.*"

In early October, just days from our impending reunion, I answered the phone to the sound of a polite voice introducing himself. "Hello, Kathe. This is your brother, Jim Chalmers."

Oh, dear God! How could this be? I puzzled. *A little brother—named Jimmy, no less—in my life after all these years?*

This was not a fluke. It was providence. This man, Jim, was my brother. I grabbed the kitchen stool and sat on it hard, groping for words, my voice trembling at the wonder of such a miracle.

"The family has just buried our mother today. She suffered a second stroke," Jim conveyed with all the care he could muster. "We found your letters and family pictures in Wilma's desk. It seems you two were planning a reunion soon. Might I suggest we go ahead with those plans? I hope you are as anxious as I am for us to meet, for I am an only kid as well, and I've always known you were out there—somewhere."

Wilma Chalmers had unwittingly brought her sweet and selfless fifty-eight-year-old son into my sixty-three-year-old life.

Our reunion in San Francisco was a smashing success. My dear, handsome brother, his wife Ginny, and their lovely daughters arrived bearing flowers and a gift album of ancestral photos. Reveling in precious snapshots of Wilma and family and tintypes of staid forbearers, we wiled away hours as Jim guided me through my legacy. How odd these ancients looked, seated and standing so stiffly. With their dreary clothes, long tresses done up in buns, beards, and stoic features, none were distinguishable from any other strangers of that era. Yet, here I was, a member in good standing, connected to ancestral dots and feeling reborn with the new knowledge that I am not Irish, as I had always surmised, but English and Scotch.

Our nieces were thrilled to have new family, and they sat in awe, watching me eat and talk. They could hardly believe I wasn't their beloved grandmother, right down to speech and hand gestures, and the sting of her death eased as we celebrated her life. Jim revealed that Wilma's four older siblings were a close bunch, and unbeknownst to Wilma, her entire family had always known about me. Our mother was the spirited one, and at sixteen had fallen prey to the amorous attentions of the local postmaster, an older and married family man. That is all I would be privileged to know of my biological father.

Never having the chance to hold Wilma's hand was a great disappointment. Jim said she had been unusually cheerful and energetic in the weeks before her death; at the time, he hadn't known why. *Could she have been relishing thoughts of our impending reunion?* I wondered.

I learn something new and fascinating about my heritage each time my brother and I burn up the phone lines. His shared knowledge and our new kinships have enriched both our lives. Filling in at least half the blank spaces in my medical records has taken away some valuable guess work between me and my doctor. As half siblings, we are in awe of the astonishing chemistry between us, grateful to unearth those similarities in the autumn of our lives rather than never at all. Inevitably, just before we call it another night of sharing news about our children and grandchildren, new and grown, Jim will regale me with another boyhood memory of the mother he adored.

Even as I continue to rediscover my roots, I will always be proud to be the person my precious parents raised me to be. I am blessed to have two loving families, one that I have cherished my life through and one that I nearly missed. My circle is complete.

—Kathe Campbell

Joshua's Baptism

We waded into the icy water of Ashland Creek with Joshua and his four hand-picked godparents. Joshua was thirteen, an age that some traditions celebrate as a transition from childhood to adulthood. We were observing a transition too: Joshua, our oldest son, was leaving home the next week for residential treatment.

Joshua chose the site for his baptism. He wanted to be baptized before our congregation in a pool below the footbridge. And he wanted to be immersed three times. So, at the point in the liturgy where the minister intones, "I baptize you in the name of God," we laid him down in the water.

He came up struggling and sputtering. "God damnit! Leave me alone!" he shouted.

"One dunking is enough," I said.

But Joshua wanted to continue. So we lowered him again.

"And in the name of Jesus Christ."

"Leave me the fuck alone!" Joshua screamed.

This time we offered to wrap up by sprinkling, rather than dunking, him. But he would go under the water again.

"And in the name of the Holy Spirit."

"Let go of me, asshole!"

We finished the baptism with a quick prayer.

The day Rich and I adopted Joshua, we met his birth mother, Angel, at her apartment, where we were set to sign the custody papers. Angel loved her two-year-old son; we never doubted that. But she suffered from mental illness and drug addiction, and she was afraid she would harm him.

A state car picked up Joshua at his foster home and delivered him to us at Angel's apartment. He ran through the door straight to his favorite toy, a plush carrot as tall as himself. Then he pulled off his shoes and dragged the carrot around by its top. The chubby, grinning toddler looked happy and healthy to Rich and me. We saw a beautiful boy with curly black hair and eyes so dark you could see yourself reflected in them. I couldn't believe he was to be ours.

When it was time to go, I picked up his shoe.

"No!" he said, pulling his foot away. I'd never been a parent before; I didn't know what to do.

Angel said, "I'll do it."

Joshua sat still for her like a puppy settling in after a romp.

Then she said, "I'll carry him to your car."

For a moment I was afraid she wouldn't be able to let go, but she tenderly settled Joshua into the new car seat and gave him a kiss. As we pulled away, Joshua was watching Angel out the rear window.

The next two years were filled with dreams that kept coming true. When my parents arrived to meet their first grandchild, Joshua took Grandpa by the hand and showed him his new bedroom. The next morning he woke them up bouncing into their bed. I have a picture of him grinning as he snuggles between them under the covers.

At four, we enrolled him in preschool. That's when it became clear that Joshua didn't behave like other children. During circle time, while the class sang, "Friends, friends, one, two, three," Joshua crawled head-first into his teacher's lap and buried his face in the folds of her skirt. He didn't want other kids looking at him. Prodded to participate, he struck a Cheshire Cat pose—his hands tucked paw-like under his chin, his lips pursed sweetly, and a wicked twinkle in his dark eyes.

"Shoo-shoo?" he murmured.

We received our first psychological assessment of Joshua when he was seven. I cried when I read it. Joshua suffered from anxiety and a disturbed sense of reality. The doctor recommended long-term psychotherapy. I felt my dream child slipping away. Still, I trusted the power of good parenting to turn him around. I was determined to stamp the demons out of him—kindly and with therapy, but stamp them out nonetheless.

By the time Joshua reached fourth grade, he was seeing a psychiatrist, counselor, special education teacher, and developmental specialist. And I had learned to expect a daily call from the school.

"Joshua's out of control. Can you come over?"

After one such call when Joshua had threatened a classmate he called "my enemy," I arrived to find him flapping like a dragonfly around a small side room. Two teachers sat with him, uselessly cajoling him to be still. I pulled him out of the room in a handcuff-hold, my fingers locked around his slender wrists, and drove him back to my office.

Upbeat and satisfied with himself, Joshua pranced ahead of me into the room, kicking off his shoes on his way through the door. I'd held my tongue in the car, but I couldn't rein in my ire a moment longer. I swept up a shoe and threw it with the fury of a harpy straight at him. He ducked. But my aim wiped the grin off his face.

"What were you thinking?" I screamed. He looked scared, watching me for further violence.

"You hate me!" he cried as he bolted past me out the door.

I gasped then at my anger and followed him. "Joshua! I'm sorry."

A pedestrian stood on the sidewalk. "He's in the bushes," the man said, indicating the ten-foot hedge that ran along the parking lot. I realized I couldn't wrestle him out of the foliage. So I retreated to the front steps and sat down.

"Joshua, please come out. I won't do it again."

It took a good ten minutes of apologizing and pleading before he crept barefoot from the hedge. I learned early of Joshua's need to reconcile after a falling out. For all the trouble he gave, he always sought proof of forgiveness afterward. I call that his saving grace.

"Why did you do that?" he whined, standing like a supplicant halfway between the hedge and the steps where I sat.

"I was really mad."

"You're not supposed to throw things at kids."

"You're right. It was wrong of me."

He sidled toward me.

"I love you more than the world," I said, using our code language.

"I love you more than life," he responded on cue.

"Come sit beside me. I'm not mad anymore."

He came. I put my arm around him, and he snuggled up against me.

If it had only been a matter of keeping Joshua at home, we would never have considered residential treatment. Rich and I had learned to gauge Joshua's moods. We could see the rise of agitation in his face, hear it in his voice. We knew how to soothe him, how to wait out his fears. School was another matter. Teachers didn't have time to sit with him until his mood passed. They wanted a program, a signal that would make him read and write and sit still. There wasn't one.

We found a residential program an hour's drive from Ashland. Joshua moved in, promising to "rip the head off" anyone who messed with him or his stuff. He thwarted three therapists in twelve months. And when that failed to get him sent home, he began running away. His first foray into the woods surrounding the facility ended after an hour. The next time he was gone a day. Then a night.

The night he disappeared, he stole a bike and rode out through the rural darkness on the shoulder of the freeway until he reached the Rogue River.

Two patrol officers spotted him, but when they approached, he jumped into the water. The officers ran down a short dock as Joshua pushed off toward a floating log. He landed on a piling beneath the bridge. The officers retreated. They didn't want to push him farther downstream. Joshua soon climbed out of the river, anyway, and hobbled to the cruiser. He'd stubbed his toe and had enough.

The clinical director suggested a more secure facility. I still expected that, once we discovered the right therapy, Joshua would be well and happy, and I would receive back the child I dreamed of. So, the August he was fourteen, uniformed guards delivered Joshua in shackles to the Oregon State Hospital in Salem, the same mental hospital where Jack Nicholson filmed *One Flew Over the Cuckoo's Nest*.

The 100-year-old buildings echoed with the whimpering of long-forgotten patients. Building C, which housed adolescents, was built of brick and concrete, a maze of wide, sterile corridors. Every door was locked, admitting only authorized staff. Alarms sounded periodically, and lights flashed. Kids lived, ate, slept, and attended therapy on the second floor. School was held in a brightly painted, but still dark, converted basement.

There was a small conference room with couches and a large window on the ground floor, where parents visited their kids. I remember one October afternoon in that room. Outside the window, a tree, planted a century ago, judging from its girth, glowed yellow in its fall foliage. Sun filtered through the leaves and warmed the couch where Joshua and I sat with our heads together. Sometimes I brought a book to read aloud. This time, the sun shining in on us made us drowsy. We packed the couch cushions and pillows around and between us and slumped into each other. The building quieted around us. I kissed Joshua's hair, and we let the drowsiness take us. Once in a while, I was aware of staff looking in on us through the open door. Just checking, I guessed.

Joshua had spent his first weeks at the hospital looking for an escape. He turned every doorknob on the chance he might find it unlocked. He used a dime to remove the cover from an air vent in his room. And when he was confined to the quiet room after a meltdown, he climbed onto a table and started pulling down the ceiling tiles.

When he gave up on escape, he tried cooperation. But it was beyond him. We began to realize that Joshua's anxiety is triggered by the stimulation of being with people. And there he was, living in a group of volatile adolescents and commanding staff. Increasingly, he dealt with his turmoil by refusing to participate. By spring, he was spending his days wrapped in a blanket, lying on the floor next to the heater.

The staff never raised the subject of releasing Joshua. I simply woke up one Saturday at home, seized by the certainty that Joshua was never going to get better in the hospital. Monday morning, I walked into Building C for his monthly review.

"I thought you weren't coming," the social worker said when she saw me.

"I changed my mind."

As staff members took their seats, piling files on the table, the social worker set a three-inch binder—eight months of Joshua's chart notes—before Dr. R., the ward psychiatrist. Dr. R. began the meeting by summing up the past month. She noted a conflict between Joshua and another boy and a few complaints Joshua had voiced about the food—he was convinced they were starving him. Then Joshua was called in, shoeless and wearing sweats.

"Mommy!" A smile lit his face. "I didn't know you were coming!"

"Surprise!" I smiled back as he sat down among the therapists.

Dr. R. asked him how he thought he was doing.

"I can't do it," he answered. "I can't go six weeks without messing up."

The psychiatrist looked puzzled, so I filled in.

"I told him what his treatment plan says, that he has to meet his behavior goals for six weeks before he can go home."

"Don't worry about that, Joshua," she said. "But you still need to try harder. You have work to do here. Do you agree?"

"Yeah." Joshua looked away.

If I had doubts about the decision Rich and I made that weekend, they were wiped away by the sadness that fell over Joshua's face. It wasn't going to be Joshua who would change. It had to be me; it had to be us; it had to be the family, the school system, the therapists.

Dr. R. sent Joshua back to his space by the heater. Then she closed the binder and prepared to wrap up the meeting.

"Wait," I said. "I have something to say."

The doctor checked her watch. "We can spend a few minutes more."

So I said, "I'm ready to let go of my dream of the child that Joshua isn't."

A month later, Rich and I brought Joshua home, as is: uncured, unchanged, unrepentant. That day we gave up trying to make him normal, to make him conform, to make him someone else. At home with a mentor and a teacher, Joshua matured on his own terms. No breakthrough therapy, no magic pill— only trial and error, time, and the bond we shared.

I could have seen on the day of his baptism what it would take to make Joshua whole. But I saw only his anxiety, heard only his sputtering and cursing. Now I understand what it meant for him to go under the water three times. That effort signified his resolve to seal the link between us.

Joshua is twenty-one now. His blustering has lessened. His anxiety has not. He still prefers to go shoeless, whatever the weather. We've battled through many missteps, both Joshua's and mine. But our hotly forged link, celebrated at his baptism, sustains us as it did that autumn afternoon in the sun-filled room when my son and I leaned into each other, dozing and dreaming.

—*Caren Hathaway Caldwell*

Like Any Other Siblings

My sister Missy, who was supposed to be a boy, arrived not in the usual way, dropped out of the sky by the stork, but via a Boeing 747.

My parents had applied for a baby boy, but Fate intervened. In the mail came a tiny black-and-white photo of an urchin, three years old. The playful way she stuck out her tongue clinched the deal. We all knew Missy was the one.

After they'd chosen the name Kimberly for her, we learned her birthday falls on Christmas Day. I argued for a name more befitting the holiday, like Chrissy Snow from the television sitcom *Three's Company*. "Kimberly" became "Missy"—short for "mistletoe."

At the airport, I watched her plane sail in like the *Mayflower*. Dad squeezed my hand, and pointing to the tarmac, proudly proclaimed, "That's not a

727, but a 747." A mere 727 wasn't good enough for our new addition. What my father had really meant was that the 727 wasn't big enough to hold Missy's personality.

That was the first time I realized I was no longer the one and only Daddy's little girl.

I squeezed hard on my dad's hand while strangers' feet shuffled on the linoleum, people coming and going all around me.

My parents argued that they'd adopted Missy so I wouldn't become a self-absorbed only child, but the real reason was so I wouldn't end up alone in a world full of strangers. With a sister, I would always have someone to hold my hand, someone who wouldn't go.

I still see that big window with the plane parked outside it, just out of reach. In my hand, I clutched a photocopied table of words the adoption agency had given us; white space created a divide between the two columns: English on the left, Vietnamese on the right.

As I waited for the first glimpse of my new sister, I held my breath, like Alice about to jump through the looking glass. Time stood still as I stood there wondering, *Would Missy like me? How would we communicate? What if I and this person, with whom I'd be sharing a room, didn't get along? Would we have to run a line of white tape down the middle of the room, like on the Brady Bunch? Why was she sticking out her tongue in that picture? Did she know about me? Had she seen my photo and decided she didn't want to be my sister?*

I was about to find out.

A woman herded the adoptive families into a conference room. The darkness contrasted with the sunlight flooding the terminal. That did not bode well.

A garbled voice announced over the loudspeaker "Pham Thi Kim," which didn't register until Dad nudged Mom to go to the podium. To me, she was already Missy.

I squinched tight, every part of me, and reminded myself to smile, just like on Christmas when I open a gift, because even if I hate it, it can't be returned. No, some presents are for life. I could tell by the nervous way Dad patted the back of my head that he was just as scared as I was that Missy would be disappointed when she unwrapped us.

Missy and I could not look more different; I knew that from the photo. Missy is as bronze as an Indian princess, while I am as pasty as a pilgrim. But I decided that I was the "native" American and she was the pilgrim. I was here first; I would stand my ground.

Mom returned with a pink bundle entwined around her torso. A small round face peered out from beneath Mom's brown curls.

Missy stretched out a tiny hand, like the tongue of a lizard, toward Dad.

Okay, she likes Dad, I thought. *And Mom. What about me?*

Missy latched her arms around Dad's neck, then snuggled into the crook of his shoulder, the way I always did. She sat on his lap the entire ride home in the station wagon, staring at me . . . like she'd won the contest. Midway through the trip, she leaned forward and vomited all over the seat between us.

What if that white space between the two columns of words could not be breached, after all, not even by a Boeing 747?

I held out the Raggedy Ann doll we'd brought for her. She clutched it to her, without letting go of Dad.

That night, Thanksgiving Eve, we camped out in the living room, silent except for the sound of Missy slurping her soup, more rice than chicken broth. Missy and I slept in our sleeping bags at perpendicular angles.

The next morning, the house cranked to life. Mom set a "children's table," complete with yellow tablecloth, by the kitchen door, so we could get used to each other, like a cat joining a family with a dog.

Mom dressed the turkey, and Dad browned the Italian sausage for his sweet potato stuffing. The can opener whirred. Dish by dish, they laid the feast on the table, just like at the original Thanksgiving: corn pudding; cranberry sauce; Dad's pumpkin pie; piquant with extra ginger; Mom's asparagus flecked with Parmesan.

I set about testing out every Vietnamese word on the list. Missy didn't say a word. Either I'd mispronounced them, or she didn't like me. Mom and Dad were less concerned with getting her to talk than to eat, her belly rounded from hunger. But even at nine, I was a writer; I dealt with words. Without words, what do we have?

Dad carried in the turkey on Mom's bone china, the fragile, careful-you-don't-break-it china, as tenuous as the connection between Missy and me. I watched him balance the platter over our heads. Not a word did he say, nor did Missy.

Missy walked over to the big table and gripped the edge, tugging on Mom's white lace tablecloth as she took in the aromatic feast spread before her. The black pepper that Dad sprinkled on everything mingled with the scent of clove-specked pie, the orange of the ambrosia, and the honey glaze of the turkey.

Butter puddled in the baked sweet potatoes Mom had forked open. I clamped the tablecloth to keep Missy from pulling everything on her head.

Dad popped the cork on the bottle of sparkling cider. The cinnamon of Mom's homemade applesauce lured Missy along the edge of the table to where Dad sat, at the head. When Missy reached up to him, he pulled her onto his lap. Sunlight poured in through the window behind him, illuminating them like the Madonna and child.

They didn't speak a word. None of us did. We didn't have to . . . because Missy smiled at me.

Last Thanksgiving, Mom landed herself in the hospital.

I race-walked down the familiar hall, soaking wet and exhausted, having got caught in the rain while shopping for Thanksgiving dinner. Missy and her husband were coming. I carried in baby wipes, hand sanitizer, juice boxes, and snacks—everything we'd forgotten in the mad dash the day before.

What had been presumed to be nothing turned out to be a blood clot, a "you have to go to the hospital now" situation. After standing by Mom's bed the day before for ten hours while she waited in the crowded hallway for a room, I got Mom settled in. I left a message for Missy, who works the night shift.

Having been kicked out of the hospital the night before at 10:45 by Nurse Ratched, I staggered into Mom's hospital room at 12:05, having been warned not to arrive before noon.

On the other side of the bed stood Missy. She'd arrived an hour earlier. Just like at the airport, she'd "won." I was nine again, displaced, the sea of white bed linens separating the two columns.

When Missy left, Mom said, "She feels left out."

"How can she feel left out?" I stammered. "She never came when Dad was in the hospital."

"She couldn't cope with it."

It's my job in the family to deal with the icky stuff. I'm the older, "serious" sibling; Missy's the social butterfly. I'm a writer; Missy has a "real" job. I'm single; she's married.

At 8:00 P.M., Nurse Ratched threw me out again. Furious—at Missy and at God—I ran-walked home in the dark. Missy, the favorite—literally, the "golden child"—had upstaged me again.

I stormed through the front door into the empty, silent house. Then it hit me. Dad's passing had taken a toll on all of us, perhaps none more than Missy. This was why Mom and Dad had adopted Missy, so I wouldn't be alone in a world of strangers when they were gone. Even though I'd assured Missy that we'd caught it early, that everything was fine, she was just as scared of losing Mom as I was. And she felt just as guilty as I did about being a dutiful daughter.

I couldn't sleep. I kept thinking about what Mom said about Missy feeling left out. But she'd made me feel left out, too.

I sat at the computer and pulled up all the old photos I'd just finished scanning. I'd made a backup copy, in case of an emergency, plus one for Missy. That was her Christmas present. Years ago, she'd confiscated a bunch of irreplaceable photos, many of Dad, without telling me. I had to reorganize the photos in new archival albums, closing the painful empty spaces where the missing photos had been.

All of our lives, our parents had insisted that they loved us "equally but differently." I was convinced it meant they loved Missy more than me. And why not? She was the chosen one; they were stuck with me. I think now they just meant they loved the things that are different about us. Being polar opposites, our differences have defined us.

But that night, last Thanksgiving, I realized just how alike we are. We're both afraid of losing Mom, like we did Dad. We tell ourselves she is the tie that binds us. But what really binds us is the fear we share of not being good enough—not good-enough daughters, not good-enough women. We share the fear of abandonment, of not being accepted and loved.

I'd been so focused on that stupid piece of paper with the two columns. It seems all our lives there has been this invisible line between us: Missy, Vietnamese; me, Caucasian. Missy, the beautiful one; me, the ugly duckling. Missy, the extrovert; me, the shy one. Missy, adopted; me, biological.

But as children we would push our beds together. Missy would reach over the divide and rest her hand on my bed as she fell asleep. Or we'd sit up and chatter until Mom called to us to go to sleep. It didn't take long for me to figure out Missy-ese—a corrupted dialect of English, an amalgam of reversed sentence structure and mixed proverbs—so I could translate to our parents what Missy was trying to communicate.

One Christmas we bought each other the same gift: a cherubic figurine carved with the words "Sometimes I Hate You, But I Always Love You." Mom had escorted us separately into the gift store, while Dad waited with the other by the mall fountain, throwing in pennies and making wishes. The coincidence pleased our parents. It proved we were just like any other pair of siblings.

There is one iconic family photo of Missy and me from our first Easter together. We're standing on the front stoop in our new Easter dresses, different colors but similar in style, organza everywhere.

Missy, literally half my size, stands turned toward me—rather than the camera—craning up, clutching a giant stuffed bunny. "Mutt and Jeff," Mom called us.

"She looks up to you," Mom still says sometimes.

How can Missy not know that I have always wanted to be just like her?

I see now that we are not so different at all. In fact, we are so much alike, it hurts.

Sometimes I hate her, but I always love her. And I know she feels the same way about me.

—*Maria Bellagrassia*

The names and some personal details of the people in this story have been changed to protect their privacy.

Magic and Miracles

hy we called it the "rag bag" I'll never know, because it certainly never held rags. My sister and I believed it contained magic and miracles. The white muslin bag was sprinkled with a sprightly pattern of blue wicker baskets overflowing with pink and yellow posies. It resided on the back porch, an alcove off the kitchen, right next to Auntie Luella's wringer washing machine. Excuse me, I mean Mama's wringer washing machine.

Even now, sixty-five years later, I still think of my adoptive mom as Auntie Luella when I recall those World War II days when we all moved into the house on Hildreth Avenue, right across the street from the South Gate Park. We weren't quite adopted yet, but Auntie Luella and Uncle Paul kept promising us a trip to court. They would be our parents after that, they said.

My big sister, Patti, and Sharon, the girl next door, would set off every morning for their first grade class. I, the five-year-old who didn't go to school yet, would mope around all morning with my Mickey Mouse coloring books and Princess Elizabeth and Princess Margaret Rose paper dolls. While I quietly played alone, I waited eagerly for them to return so we could take up our afternoon adventure, which always involved rummaging through the contents of that singular sack, the rag bag.

Playing dress-up was our favorite pastime. We could become gypsy princesses, brides, nurses, ballerinas, or even Wonder Woman through the artful draping of a lace curtain or the donning of a pair of Mama's frayed satin step-ins. There was even an old feather duster that we could transform into a scepter or a wand.

One rainy afternoon while we sorted through the discards and remnants, I asked Patti and Sharon about court and what that meant. They exchanged wise and knowing glances and mentioned that kings and queens lived in castles. I knew that. I had a fairy tale book of my own. But what was court?

Patti plucked a beaded necklace from the rag bag and draped it around her forehead. "Well, I'll show you," she said, "I am the queen, and you all are my ladies-in-waiting, my court." She swept her arm about imperiously, as if the miniscule niche were a huge hall packed with her minions. "Now curtsy."

I looked expectantly at Sharon, who plucked up the corners of her skirt, lowered her curly blond head, crooked her right ankle behind her left, and bowed. When I imitated her, I overdid the forward tilt and smacked the linoleum with my forehead.

Auntie Luella bustled back from the kitchen when she heard my yowls. Kneeling beside me, she wiped my tears with a corner of her apron and frowned at my sister.

"We were teaching her to curtsy. We're just getting ready for court," Patti explained.

"Yes," Sharon chimed in, "so she won't be embarrassed."

"Why would she be embarrassed?" Auntie Luella seemed perplexed.

"Well, she's just a little girl. She doesn't know much yet, since she hasn't been to school," Patti explained. Sharon nodded assent.

"She doesn't need to know much more than to tell the judge her name," Auntie Luella said.

"What's a judge?" I asked. "I thought I was going to court to see a queen."

Auntie Luella sighed. "There are no queens at adoption court, but there will be a judge who will ask if you want to stay here with us."

Our day in court arrived soon. On her pedal sewing machine, Grandma ran up a pair of sheer, dotted swiss dresses with wide ribbon belts, mine pale pink and Patti's baby blue. When Patti helped me tie the bow, she said we looked like princesses. I wondered if the judge would wear a crown like a king.

The court itself didn't look at all like the pictures of palace interiors I had seen in my story books. It looked more like church, with rows of dark wooden benches.

I tugged at Auntie Luella's hand. "Where's the king?" I whispered.

"It's a judge, and here he comes," she whispered back, pointing toward a door in the front of the room.

He didn't look much like Old King Cole to me. He wore a robe, but it was black, not red, and there was no fur around the lapels. And he wore glasses, just like Grandpa's, and no crown covered his bald head. Tears of disappointment welled up in my eyes, and I instinctively thrust my thumb into my mouth to keep from sobbing aloud.

"Will Paul and Luella French come forward and bring their new daughters, Patti and Terri?" the judge asked in a deep sonorous voice. He sounded just like the announcer on the radio show, *The Shadow*, who said, "Who knows what evil lurks in the hearts of men?" When I would hear those introductory words, I always ran from the room to escape the blood-curdling laugh that followed.

I started to shiver, but we all shuffled forward, an awkward quartet, me clinging to Auntie Luella's skirt. She reached down and gently tugged my thumb from my mouth. I looked up and then remembered that I had to curtsy. Patti rolled her eyes when I dipped, but the judge smiled.

"I see you have very good manners," he said. Then he talked for a while with Auntie Luella and Uncle Paul before turning his attention back to us. Finally, he told my sister that now that she was adopted she had to promise to practice her piano scales every day.

Then he turned to me. "Terri, I understand that you are afraid of water running in the bathtub and sink," he said. That was the truth, so I decided he must be able to read my mind. "You have to promise to wash behind your ears every day." The tears I had been holding back came gushing forward.

The rest of the afternoon remains a blur. I remember coming home to find Sharon from next door waiting on the front porch. Patti and I traded our party dresses for our usual shirts and shorts, and we all rushed to the rag bag to reenact the day. Patti found an old overcoat to turn herself into the judge. Sharon played Auntie Luella, tottering about in a pair of high-heeled sandals. I played myself, curtsying and sniffling.

As evening began to fall, after Sharon returned home, Auntie Luella joined us on the back porch with a tray of lemonade and ginger snaps. As we munched, she asked us what we remembered about the day.

"I have to practice scales," Patti responded.

"Oh, Auntie Luella," I moaned, "I have to wash behind my ears."

She smiled and shook her head. "Girls, you forgot the most important thing that the judge said today."

We stared at her blankly. I couldn't think of anything other than that he knew about how running water triggered alarms.

"It's that you have to call us Mama and Daddy from now on. No more Auntie Luella or Uncle Paul."

She reached into the rag bag and pulled out the feather duster. "This is my magic wand," she said, flourishing it before us. "Now, you're my daughters and I'm your mother."

Patti nodded. I curtsied.

It's been a while since I've seen my big sister. I hope we'll get together soon. I plan to ask her whether, after all these decades, she still follows her edict and practices her scales. I will reassure her that I still wash behind my ears. And I'll inquire if she still remembers that white muslin rag bag, crammed with magic and miracles.

—*Terri Elders*

Are You His Mother?

Busy inside the house, I didn't hear the brakes squeal or the shouts, but somehow I knew from the frantic pounding on the front door that there had been another disaster and our son Nick was in the middle of it—again.

"Where's your phone?" the young man blurted as I opened the door. His face was pale, and it wasn't just the lack of a summer tan. I knew he had run to our house because it was the closest one to Becker School, where Nick attended first grade. What I didn't yet know was how close we came to losing Nick that day.

"In the kitchen!" Frantic to be out the door and on my way to Nick, I yanked the young man inside, gesturing toward the kitchen and our blue princess phone. It was 1977, and cell phones didn't exist.

At six, Nick was a whirling dervish of a kid. Because of his hyperactive behavior, he'd already been ejected from preschool and Sunday school. Kindergarten hadn't gone too well, either, but luckily, this year he'd landed in Mrs. Ferrini's first grade. She saw him as a high-energy gifted child rather than as a problem, and he responded by giving her bragging rights to a student who scored at the high school level in reading, science, and language.

We had adopted Nick at two months, knowing his prenatal background included alcohol and drugs. There wasn't much information available, and what the social worker did share seemed implausible, especially the part about his nineteen-year-old-father being in med school.

As soon as he could toddle, Nick kept us in shape chasing after him in parking lots, retrieving him from the giant fir tree in our yard, and sprinting up department store stairs to intercept the elevator he'd climbed aboard. We'd taken several trips to the emergency room, and as I tore out the door, praying the young man had located the phone, I suspected that Nick and I might be on our way there again.

Near the corner, a circle of onlookers in bright spring clothing surrounded something about the size of a six-year-old lying in the street. Nearby, an older sedan had come to a halt with one wheel up on the curb.

I pushed my way through the crowd and confirmed what my heart already knew. The object in the street was Nick. The crowd shifted back as I dropped down on the warm asphalt, held Nick's head and talked to him. He seemed aware of me but didn't answer. I watched as his small chest rose and fell, each breath bracketed by a peculiar whistling sound.

Around me, I could hear the crowd's worried murmuring, "He isn't crying." *But, of course,* I thought. *They know nothing of Nick and his resilience.*

As I knelt in the street, the crowd parted in a wave that exposed the lady who had driven the car. She huddled against the driver's door, weeping silently into a handkerchief. She was about the age of Nick's grandmother.

I flinched as an older gentleman touched my shoulder. He held out Nick's shoe, explaining that he'd picked it up some ten feet away. Oddly, he offered me advice on shoe care, "I think a little polish will clean it right up."

I turned back to my son, continuing to study each breath, straining to hear the wail of the approaching sirens. I knew not to move Nick but nothing more helpful. It seemed like a year before the ambulance arrived, spilling attendants from every door. They moved toward us in sync, deftly excluding me as they formed a barrier of bodies and equipment around Nick.

While most of the paramedics worked on Nick, the youngest appeared to have been assigned to me. I looked up as he squatted next to me, so close that I could smell his cologne and read that his name was "Erik." The other paramedics moved quickly and efficiently through their routines while Erik and I sat unmoving and silent, elbows touching. I thought it a peculiar sort of camaraderie, but maybe not. I had no experience in this.

Finally, it was time to load Nick and get to the hospital. But when I rose to follow Nick into the ambulance, Erik's purpose became clear. He reached out and grasped my arm. "Do you know how to reach his mother?"

I looked down at his hand—the one stopping me from entering the ambulance with my son. "I'm his mother," I said, watching his eyes widen in surprise.

Once again, I had forgotten that I am white and Nick is black.

Nick survived his encounter with the car, and life ran smoothly for awhile.

Then came middle school, raging hormones, and racism—a formidable combination. Neither Nick nor our family self-destructed during those years only because of school counselor Hap Swenson and the extra hours he added to his already overcrowded schedule. During the day, Hap struggled to civilize 300 middleschoolers. At home in the evening, he contacted the parents of Nick's classmates, most of whom had the grace to be appalled by the racist antics of their offspring. Nick took it all in stride, using his gift of humor when he could and his fists when he had to. By the end of eighth grade, everyone at the track meet knew that the white couple cheering for Nick were his parents. I rarely heard, "Are you his mother?"

When serious dating started in high school, gregarious Nick found himself isolated by the color of his skin. By graduation he'd had enough of small-town life in Oregon, and he followed his dream to join the military. Because he was only seventeen, parental consent was necessary. I thought it ironic that the recruiter, eager to make his quota, didn't question whether I was his mother.

Time passed as the Marines sent Nick around the world: Somalia, Cambodia, Germany, Bahrain, and, finally, Iraq, where he serves as an explosive ordnance disposal (EOD) tech, defusing roadside bombs, missiles, and other devices that are extraordinarily destructive to human flesh.

The news from Iraq grows worse each day. I can't read the newspaper. My favorite TV show, *NewsHour with Jim Lehrer*, ends with a silent roll call of young men and women who are no more. I reflect that each of their mothers sent off a child and, in return, received a flag-draped box.

My world is upside-down with worry about Nick. I send large boxes of cookies, paperbacks, and photos, which he shares with his buddies. If any of them notice that I am white and Nick is black, none seem to care.

At night, I am unable to close my eyes without scenes of violence playing behind my eyelids. On the worst nights, the film moves in slow motion. I see myself standing, head bowed, beside one of many wooden boxes. My hand rests lightly atop the flag. Around me, shadowy figures observe my grief. No one asks, "Are you his mother?"

—*Ange Crawford*

Author's note: Nick returned safely from Iraq and is currently stationed at Twentynine Palms, California.

The Holes of a Child's Heart

"We need to talk after the service," Jancsi said, catching us in the hallway as we arrived at church. "Marian, the orphanage director, wants me translate this letter for you. It's about Niki's health. Something you need to know about." Jancsi handed me the letter as he rushed off and began tuning his guitar in preparation for church.

I clutched the small envelope in my hand and looked at the scribbled Hungarian handwriting addressing it. *What now?* I thought to myself as I pulled out the letter.

We had already been hit with the child's endless litany of health ailments: Severe food allergies, requiring a strict diet and medication administered five times a day. Scoliosis, requiring daily use of a back brace and therapy. A severe overbite that would eventually require surgery. And, perhaps most frightening, a hole in her heart, the ramifications of which were still unclear to us. What else could be wrong?

I didn't want to sit through the service. I just wanted to pour over the obscure combination of letters and accent marks that filled the page in my hand and try to make sense of it. But it was no use. My Hungarian had not progressed past the simplest of conversation. This was technical Hungarian—a doctor's evaluation of some sort. There was nothing to do but wait. The songs of the service droned on. I was in no mood to worship. The long sermon began, but I did not listen. All I could think about was what else could be wrong with little Niki.

Finally, the service ended and the chit-chat of postservice socializing began. *"Sziasztok!"* I greeted Hungarian friends with feigned enthusiasm as my husband and I worked our way up through the crowd toward Jancsi.

An ethnic Hungarian, Jancsi was a long-time friend who had worked painstakingly with us organizing programs and special events for the Hungarian orphanages since before we'd moved to Hungary to do that kind of work full-time. After we'd met Niki and determined to adopt the blue-eyed, five-year-old, he had served as our compass, helping us to navigate the treacherous sea of Hungarian adoption bureaucracy.

We settled at a small table in the church coffee bar. I handed Jancsi the letter, and we leaned in to hear so that we could hear him translate amidst the sounds of various small groups of people chatting.

"This is Niki's most recent mental and psychological evaluation," Jancsi explained first. "Marian thought it only right that you know everything before you complete the adoption."

The letter revealed Niki lagged in much of her mental development, possibly due to fetal alcohol syndrome. Her small and large motor skills ranked below her age group as did her language skills. She also showed signs of possible mental retardation—the extent of which could not be fully determined. The doctor recommended that these issues could best be dealt with in a foster home or adoptive family setting.

My heart plummeted headlong into my stomach as I looked at my husband, Russell. Niki was already ours in my heart. These issues could not change that. But I grieved to know she faced such struggles. And how did Russell feel about it?

My husband let out a long sigh. "So?" He threw up his hands and looked at Jancsi.

"The officials thought it important that you know this in case it changes your decision to adopt

Niki," our friend explained in his trademark patient manner.

Russell shook his head. His almond-shaped eyes flashed the way they do when he gets his back up. "Of course, this does not change anything!" he announced, somewhat incensed. He leaned back in the chair as his volume increased with agitation. "Why are we wasting our time with these letters and this bureaucracy when experts are saying she needs to be in a home now and out of the orphanage?"

The Hungarian social system had classified Niki as "extremely hard to place." It was a classification based purely on how the five-year-old looked on paper. How many people would choose to adopt a nameless, faceless child with such a litany of physical and possibly mental challenges? How tragic that all these ailments would so readily drive potential parents away in droves. Perhaps, deep down in her frail, little soul, that rejection proved to be her greatest ailment of all, the biggest hole in her heart.

But to us Niki was more than medical records and physician evaluations. She was the blue-eyed, brown-haired bundle of affection that had stolen our family's hearts—starting with our biological daughter's.

Six months earlier, I had been sifting through digital pictures from one of our orphanage programs while our four-year-old, Andi, danced around my chair. She peeked over my shoulder to see what I was doing just as Niki's picture popped up on the computer screen.

"I know her. She's my friend!" Andi announced. Indeed, they had played together during the event at which the photo had been taken.

I pulled Andi up into my lap, and we stared at the photo. The little girl seemed to look back at us from the computer screen through her crystal blue, almost melancholy eyes. "I know she is, sweetheart," I said. "Her name is Niki, but I do not think she has a mommy or daddy."

Andi thought for a moment. Her four-year-old consciousness could not fully absorb what such a tragedy meant. But she is a problem-solver, nonetheless. "Well," she said, the wheels in her young brain clearly turning, "you and Daddy could be her mom and dad."

That had started it all.

Throughout the nine-month adoption process, Niki's health issues steadily fell upon us like persistent bombs. We could only speculate how all these challenges would affect our family life.

Then the fateful day finally arrived. Niki was coming home. With a two-and-a-half inch thick stack of medical records and files, we loaded her into our van at the orphanage and headed to our house. Our minds raced. *Given her special needs, how long would it take her to learn English? Did I get all the instructions for medications down correctly? What if she eats something she is allergic to? And what about that hole in her heart?*

"Mommy, I'm hungry," Andi yelled from the back of the van, taking a break from the mantra of Hungarian chatter and giggles with her new sister.

"We will eat as soon as we get home," I told her and then continued talking with my husband and Jancsi, who had come with us.

"Mommy, I'm thirsty," Andi interrupted again.

"We will be home soon, sweetie," I assured her, and the girls went back to their preschool banter, which sounds roughly the same in any language.

"Mommy!" I turned to see what Andi wanted this time, but the cry had not come from Andi.

Niki's lips parted into big grin as she again said, "Mommy," and then mumbled something in Hungarian.

Was she simply imitating Andi's words, or did she grasp what was happening on some level? I couldn't know for sure, but less than an hour after taking her in, she was calling me "Mommy" and doing it in English!

Within three months, Niki was conversant in English, artfully using phrases like, "But Mommy,

Andi started it!" Could this be the same child who lagged in language skills in her native tongue?

During those first couple of months, mealtime always simmered with stress, and Niki sensed it. Food had always brought her misery as caregivers agonized over her meals, ever fearing adverse allergic consequences. With the New Year, we had Niki retested for food allergies. The result: a single allergy, to kiwi fruit.

All the medications went in the trash and a whole new epicurean world opened up for Niki. We watched with delight as she discovered ice cream for the first time in her life. By the time she'd finished, the sweet, frosty treat covered the lower half of her mouth, like giant pink clown's lips, accentuating her already unforgettable smile. Her menu expanded to include milk, cheese, eggs, carrots, and soy—all the things she once had to avoid. Surprisingly, the Hungarian orphan's favorite food proved to be the quintessential American classic—macaroni and cheese.

Her allergies had mysteriously disappeared. Some doctors said perhaps she'd outgrown them. Others suggested she was originally misdiagnosed. But the fact remained, they were gone.

All the other fears faded quickly as well. The child, although easily distracted, had a keen mind and an ear for languages. Still, the most foreboding of ailments haunted us—the hole in her heart. I made an appointment to have it reevaluated at a local Hungarian hospital.

The medical complex sprawled out before us like a morose forest of ugly concrete buildings. Here, the maze of Hungarian bureaucracy became tangible as Niki and I wandered from one dank, colorless building to another, stopping people along the way to ask for directions in my flailing Hungarian.

After stumbling Niki through an EKG, I dragged her across the vast campus in search of the section of the hospital that handles ultrasonography. The cardiologist, a pleasant woman in her thirties, greeted us with a kind smile and the welcome sound of English words. She set Niki up on the table and rubbed the gel on her chest.

"Is it going to hurt?" Niki asked fearfully in Hungarian.

"No," the woman smiled as she answered. "This doesn't hurt at all. We are just taking pictures."

She chatted with Niki as she ran the sonogram machine over the child's chest and studied the screen.

"Hmmm, that's interesting," she said, as she helped Niki change positions to try a new angle . . . and then another. "Well, I am not finding any indication of a hole." She then looked at the EKG taken that morning. "The EKG is perfect, too." The cardiologist smiled. "The problem she had seems to have cleared itself up. That happens sometimes."

As I thanked the doctor and scurried Niki back to get dressed, I found myself a little bit awestruck. It was like a miracle—a whole series of miracles. All those things that had made Niki "extremely hard to place" had vanished like the night's frightening shadows in the light of a new day.

A new day had, indeed, dawned. Rejected by so many and written off by the system, Niki, the melancholy-eyed orphan emerged as our blue-eyed bundle of delight, full of health, life, and love.

Sometimes, the love of family—more so than pills and procedures—is the best medicine, serving as a healing salve to the wounds of the body as well as to the spirit. And, sometimes, love can even fill the holes of a child's broken heart.

—*Trudy Chun*

Finding Me: A Bedtime Story

People sometimes ask me, "How did you come to find out you were adopted?"

"Through a nightly bedtime story told to me as a little boy," I reply. "And somehow, through that repeated narrative, I came to gradually understand and accept that I was a preferred child chosen to be part of a loving family."

As far back as I can remember, my adopted mother would sit next to my bed in the evening, tuck me in, and tell me a story to help me go to sleep. I suffered from long bouts of insomnia during most of my childhood, and it seemed that the only remedy to appease those restless fits was her quiet, soothing voice just before surrendering to my dreams.

Even before I understood what it meant to be adopted, I was told nightly of a hard-working husband and wife who longed to have another child.

Early on in their marriage, the woman had bore a healthy son. Later on, however, she suffered a miscarriage. And then another. And another. Finally, she was told by the family physician that she could never have children again.

The father and mother both yearned for a solution that would bring another child into their home. Not only did they want their only son to have a sibling to look after, they also wanted to give a little baby a solid upbringing with lots of devoted attention and care. So they put in a request at an official agency for children needing safe homes. Eventually, and over a period of months, a social worker came to the family's house to make sure the living situation for the potential child was comfortable and welcoming.

"Was it hard to find the right baby?" I'd ask.

"The family waited a very long time," I distinctly remember my adopted mother replying. "But finally, the most perfect, beautiful, blue-eyed baby boy came to live in their home, and he was the fulfillment of all of their hopes and desires."

At this point in the story, I recollect that, as I grew a little older, I began to ask questions. I wanted to know more about the little baby son who had come to live with the family. Patiently, my adopted mother would answer each and every question.

As the portrait of the little boy became clearer, I began to see that we had quite a bit in common. We both loved to ride our bicycles until the streetlamps came on. We both loved to eat strawberry gelatin with grapes suspended inside of it. And most of all, we both had a desire to sing all of the time.

"Does he know all the songs from *Mary Poppins* just like me?" I asked one evening.

"Just like you!"

"Do you think I'll ever meet him?" I wondered out loud.

"We'll have to see what happens in the next chapters," she would wink.

Night after night, I heard more features about the life of the child who was brought into the home. My mother would make an ordinary ranch house in the suburbs sound like a fairy-tale castle, with tales of sweeping Midwestern tornados and vast cornfields that seemed to encroach upon the little subdivision. Everything in the story had a ring of familiarity to it but was tinged with the mysterious and exotic.

One particularly restless evening when I was seven years old, I asked my mother to tell me the story of the orphaned child. I wanted to know specifically where he came from.

"No one is really certain where he came from," she began very deliberately. "Catholic Charities brought him to the home but said the records of his birth parents must remain sealed."

"So he'll never be able to find out?" I asked with a peaked curiosity.

"His true identity must remain a secret, but the parents who raise him now hope that he will understand that what's most important is how much he is wanted and needed."

"So he really is loved, after all?"

"Oh, he is cherished more than you can ever imagine," she emphatically stressed.

After a while, she handed me a cup of warm milk to drink, and we sat together quietly as I drank it. I remember it was summertime and still light out, and even after the story, I didn't feel I could go to sleep.

So I asked, "Where does the little baby live now?"

"He lives right here with us."

I remember so well her drawn-in breath and the heartbeat pause that lingered between sentences as she brought her face closely to my own. "He writes poems and makes up little songs, and he's growing up to be a very smart, handsome, and talented little boy."

That's when I found myself in her story. I recognized then that the beloved baby was really, in fact, me. At only seven years old, I comprehended that the family that had waited so long to care for a child was the family I was living with right then, my very own family.

The discovery in that moment came over me in gentle waves and has continued to offer me solace over the years. Later, as a teen, I came to ask more questions about my uncertain origins, which, to this day, are still shielded by restrictive privacy laws. But as a child growing up, I felt an essential foundation was in place because I understood that I was the protagonist in a profound love story and I had truly been desired.

Now, as an adult, when I sometimes cannot find sleep, I remind myself of that magical childhood fable told to me night after night. I hear my mother's soft voice as she gently unravels the tale of the baby boy who was sought after, waited upon, and chosen to inherit not only the family's last name, but more important, their story of realized dreams, their legacy of love.

—Gerard Wozek

Contributors

Maria Bellagrassia ("Like Any Other Siblings") is the pseudonym of a freelance writer who hails from the northeastern United States. She earned a master's degree in English literature and loves to write.

Gaye Brown ("Ready or Not . . ."), who lives in Maryland, is a former director of publishing for the Smithsonian Institution's American Art Museum and National Museum of the American Indian. She subsequently served as a writer and researcher for Time-Life's history series *What Life Was Like*. Her work has appeared in the *Georgetown Review*, *Nathaniel Hawthorne Review*, and *Washington Review*.

Sallie Wagner Brown ("My *Own* Mother!") writes stories inspired by her kids, who think they are grown up, by her dogs, who think they are her kids, and by the old Douglas firs surrounding her Corvallis, Oregon, home. She retired from teaching English at age fifty and bought a used, red Corvette. She knows she isn't grown up.

Jeff Buppert ("To Be Chosen") has been a butler for two governors, a game show contestant, and a steer wrestler, but he is now a freelance writer living in Los Angeles whose work has appeared in print, on the Web, and on stage. A columnist for the online salon, Mad as HELL Club, he is currently working on a book to help children deal with the loss of a pet.

Caren Hathaway Caldwell ("Joshua's Baptism") has been a teacher, reporter, social worker, organizer, and for the past twenty-three years an ordained minister of the United Church of Christ. She lives in Ashland, Oregon, with her partner, Rich Rohde, a community organizer, and their two adopted sons, now seventeen and twenty-one. A community activist, she advocates throughout Southern Oregon for children with mental illness and their parents.

Kathe Campbell ("Never Too Late") lives on a Montana mountain with her mammoth donkeys, a Keeshond, and a few kitties. A prolific writer on Alzheimer's, she has published stories in medical journals, magazines, e-zines, and anthologies, including the *Cup of Comfort®* book series and *RX for Writers*.

Jean Campion ("The Outlaws"), author of the historical novels *Minta Forever* and *Return to Rockytop*, taught writing at Fort Lewis College in Durango, Colorado, for fifteen years. She is a regular contributor to the *Cup of Comfort®* book series, and her work has appeared in numerous other publications. She has three children and a new grandson.

Trudy Chun ("The Holes of a Child's Heart") is a writer, mother of two, and missionary living in Eastern Hungary. She and her family work with GoodSports International, a nonprofit organization that uses sports programs to reach out to underprivileged children. Before entering the mission field, she served as editor of *Family Voice* magazine and as a contributor to *Breakpoint WorldView* magazine.

J.M. Cornwell ("Amanda's Seeds") is a nationally syndicated freelance writer, editor, award-winning author, and book reviewer. Her work has appeared widely, including *New Woman* magazine, the *New York Times*, *Haunted Encounters: Departed Family and Friends*, and several *Cup of Comfort®* anthologies. She lives among ghosts and books in a Victorian in the Colorado Rockies.

Ange Crawford ("Are You His Mother?") lives with her family in Oregon's mid-Willamette Valley. After a career in juvenile justice, she made the change to children's book author, freelance writer, grant writer, and avid community volunteer. Her work appears in books, magazines, journals, anthologies, and newspapers worldwide. Ange was recently honored by Oregon Writers Colony for her nonfiction.

Terri Elders ("Magic and Miracles"), LCSW, lives near Colville, Washington, with her husband, Ken Wilson, two dogs, and three cats. She serves as a federal grant reviewer and public member of the Washington State Medical Commission. Her tales have appeared in several anthologies, including A *Cup of Comfort*® *for New Mothers*.

Jerri Farris ("Flossy, Flossy") is the author of twenty-two books on home décor, home improvement, and crafts. She lives in Independence, Missouri, on the banks of a pond known affectionately to her family as "Lake Not-So-Much." She is absurdly proud of the people her children, Evan and Katie, have become.

Debra Feintech ("Invisible Bonds") works as a counselor and shamanic practitioner in Portland, Maine. She lives with her family in an old, rambling farmhouse that supports her passion for family, gardening, Spirit, and sacred space.

Lois Gerber ("The Woman with the Long, Auburn Hair") has been a community health nurse for more than thirty-five years. Presently, she lives in Florida and does volunteer work with teen mothers and the state's foster-child program. Her stories and articles have appeared in numerous parenting, nursing, and regional women's magazines.

Kim Gonzalez ("Scenes from the Broken Road"), who is both an adoptee and an adoptive mom, lives in rural Wisconsin with her husband, daughter, and two cats. A freelance copyeditor, when she's not working on or reading a good book, she enjoys cooking, gardening, and jogging.

Betty Hard ("That Saucy One") lives in Orillia, Ontario, Canada, where, at age eighty-one, she still enjoys gardening, crafting, and performing with The Entertainers music and dance troupe. After participating in a writing workshop at the local public library, she penned "That Saucy One," her first published piece. She is now writing her memoirs as a legacy for her five grandchildren and three great-grandchildren.

Linda Darby Hughes ("He Has Her Hands, but They Hold My Heart") is a freelance writer and editor living in Douglasville, Georgia. Her articles and stories on faith and family have appeared in numerous magazines, newspapers, and anthologies, including *A Cup of Comfort® for Christians* and *A Cup of Comfort® Book of Prayer.*

Randi Israelow ("Aglow with Gratitude") was adopted at birth thanks to a newspaper article on adoption. She has worked at St. Martin's Press, Capitol Records, Word Records, and FM Global. She has written country music reviews for *NuCity* newsmagazine (Albuquerque, New Mexico) as well as patient and family stories for Alive Hospice, a nonprofit organization in Nashville, Tennessee. Randi attends a weekly writers circle in Burbank, California.

Kim Johnson ("Are You Adopted?") is the executive secretary to the vice president/general counsel at Disneyland as well as a public speaker and a column editor for an online newsletter. Her work appears in several compilations, and her book, *Working Women's Devotions to Go.* Residing in Anaheim, California, she and her husband have a blended family of four children and five grandchildren.

Ruth E. Jones ("An Answer, Without Question"), a graduate of Northwestern University, has been a practicing physical therapist for more than twenty-seven years and currently shares her healing therapies at John Knox Village retirement center in Tampa, Florida. Her essays have appeared in the Healing Project's *Voices of Alzheimer's* anthology and the *St. Petersburg Times.*

Annie Kassof ("Black and White") is a freelance writer. After publishing more than a dozen essays on adoption and foster care in publications such as the *Los Angeles Times* and *Adoptive Families* magazine, she is now branching out in her writing to include subject matters such as mule-riding and depression. She lives in Berkeley, California, with her teenage birth son and twelve-year-old transracially adopted daughter.

Jean Kinsey ("Billy's Prayer"), a widow and retired Realtor, lives in Brooks, Kentucky. She enjoys traveling, camping, and teaching Sunday school. Her award-winning writing has appeared in multiple anthologies and many inspirational periodicals. She is in the process of writing an inspirational historical novel.

Susan R. Kostuch ("The Journey to Me") lives with her husband, children, and animals at Rocky Mountain House, Alberta, Canada. After spending ten years working in the field of human services, she is now a homemaker and aspiring writer. She enjoys hiking, camping with her family, archaeology, gardening, and environmental stewardship.

Marybeth Lambe ("Yuanjun's Home") lives with her husband and seven children on their small farm outside Seattle, Washington. When she is not chasing children or chickens, Marybeth works as a physician and a writer.

Helen Legocki ("The Zit") and her husband, Tony, welcomed their son, Sam, home from Korea two years after the arrival of their daughter, Mary Kate. After raising their family in Albany, New York, the couple retired to The Villages, Florida. Helen has been active in the Compassionate Friends, a self-help group for bereaved parents, and in the now-defunct International Adoptive Families.

Donna Morin Miller ("Meant to Be") is a freelance writer who lives outside of Boston with her husband and son. When not reading or writing, she enjoys spending time with her family, hiking through the woods, and sampling new vegetarian recipes. She can't imagine her life without the little boy who was truly meant to be.

Judy Miller ("Souls Speak") is an Indiana-based freelance writer. She is a proud mom to her blended brood of adopted and biological children. She has been published in a variety of parenting magazines.

Lad Moore ("Particularly Close to His Granny"), of Woodlawn, Texas, is a multiple contributor to the *Cup of Comfort®* book series. He has published more than 600 works, including three short story collections of his own. He received third place in the 2000 Raymond Carver Short Fiction contest (sponsored by the University of Washington) and was a Best Short Fiction nominee for the 2001 Texas Institute of Letters' contest.

Barbara Mountjoy ("The Good, the Tough, and the Mommy") has been a writer for more than thirty-five years and has raised seven kids, including three special-needs children. Her most recent credits also include *101 Little Instructions for Surviving Your Divorce* and a story in *A Cup of Comfort® for Divorced Women*. She works as a family law attorney in northwestern Pennsylvania.

Lindee Nearmy ("The Real Deal") lives on the mid-coast of Adelaide, South Australia, with her husband and three daughters. Currently a stay-at-home mum, she holds bachelor's degrees in art and in education. Her short stories and articles have appeared in *Readers Digest, Story Station, That's Life!, Comet,* and *Explore* magazines.

Christina S. Nelson ("Kissed by an Angel") lives with her husband and four kids on a small farm in Oregon's beautiful Willamette Valley. She is involved in homeschooling activities and teaches classes to homeschool groups in the area. She is the author of *A Typical Summer for Lilly McGilly* (Oaktara Publishers, spring 2009).

Deesha Philyaw ("The Talk: Part One in a Series") is a freelance writer who has written for *Essence, Bitch,* and *Wondertime* magazines and the *Washington Post*. Her writing has been anthologized in *Just Like a Girl: A Manifesta!* and *Literary Mama: Reading* for the Maternally Inclined. A native of Jacksonville, Florida, she lives in Pittsburgh with her daughters.

Jessica Pierce ("A Good Mom") holds a bachelor's degree in writing and English literature from Oglethorpe University. A freelance writer, she lives in Atlanta, Georgia, and enjoys cooking and gardening.

Victoria Roder ("Why I Believe in Angels"), the director for Zion Lutheran Daycare, lives in Spencer, Wisconsin, with her husband, Ron, and a houseful of pets. Her first novel, *The Dream House*, is to be released spring 2009, and her articles and puzzles have appeared in several magazines.

Pamela Schoenewaldt ("Near Brazigovo") teaches professional and fiction writing at the University of Tennessee, Knoxville. Her short stories have been published in the United States, England, France, and Italy, winning the Chekhov Award for Short Fiction (given by the *Crescent Review*) and the Leslie Garrett Short Fiction Award (given by the Knoxville Writers Guild), as well as awards from the Tennessee Writers Alliance and the Writers Place. Another account of her older-child adoption appears in *The Movable Nest: A Mother/Daughter Companion*.

John Sonego ("His Gift and His Burden") and his partner, Michael Arden, adopted three brothers, Dereck, Michael, and Matthew, in July 2004. The two dads, three brothers, and their three dogs, live in Hollywood, California.

Liz Tolsma ("As American as They Come" and "Simply His Mother") is the pseudonym of a freelance writer who shares a home in Wisconsin with her husband and their three internationally adopted children, whom she homeschools. A graduate of Trinity Christian College, she taught second grade before leaving to start a family and pursue her writing career.

Kali VanBaale ("A Tale of Two Names" and "Russian Lullaby") lives outside Des Moines with her husband and three children. Her debut novel, *The Space Between*, earned a 2007

American Book Award, the 2007 Independent Publisher's silver medal for general fiction, and the 2006 Fred Bonnie Memorial Award for Best First Novel. Her short story "Behind Lace Curtains" appeared in the 2007 anthology *Voices of Alzheimer's*.

Samantha Ducloux Waltz ("Special Sisters") is an award-winning writer in Portland, Oregon. Her essays can be seen in numerous anthologies, including several in the *Cup of Comfort®* book series. Her beloved sister lives in Parowan, Utah, with her husband, surrounded by relatives and friends.

Marian Webster ("What Matters Most") began writing at sixty-seven, after her husband's death. Now seventy-six, she has published stories in *Progenitor 2003* magazine (Arapahoe Community College), *Classic Christmas: True Stories of Holiday Cheer and Goodwill*, and *Miracles of Kindness*. Marian currently lives with her son in Colorado but plans to grow old back home in Arizona.

Christine White ("Don't Eat My Birth Mother") is a freelance writer and stay-at-home feminist living in New England with her husband, daughter, and their cat. She has written for *Adoption Today* magazine and worked at an international adoption agency for a few years before becoming a parent.

Gerard Wozek ("Finding Me: A Bedtime Story") is a resident of Naperville, Illinois. He teaches literature and the humanities at Robert Morris College in Chicago. He is currently writing a memoir about growing up in a closed adoption.

About the Editor

Colleen Sell has compiled thirty volumes of the *Cup of Comfort*® book series; authored, ghostwritten, and edited numerous books; published scores of articles and essays; and served as editor-in-chief of two award-winning magazines. She and her husband, T.N. Trudeau, live in a turn-of-the-century farmhouse on a forty-acre pioneer homestead in the Pacific Northwest. She is blessed with a large, loving, creative, compassionate Irish family as well as many dear friends whom she has unofficially adopted as family.